# THE BUSINESS OF REDEMPTION

"Leadership starts and ends with ownership; and is driven by a passion for positive change. James takes full ownership of his life and the events that lead to regrettable and tragic loss of life. Nothing can undo that or make it better. But James example of choosing to own his circumstance, choosing to give a full and brutally honest accounting, choosing to stand back up, choosing to give and live life fully again is a great example. I recommend this book to everyone and especially for those whose ambition drives them to lead and make the world a better place. We can all learn from what James has to share."

—**John Quigley**, Vice President of Research and Development, NXP Semiconductors

"In 2009, we were developing a television project with James. He was on top of the world, and the networks loved him. Then his entire world collapsed. It was the most stunning turnaround; and devastating to watch as he lost everything— his home, his career, his partner, most of his friends, and his freedom. *The Business of Redemption* is wonderfully written, gripping, and told with incredible honesty and humility. It is a true testimony to how life can be rebuilt, even from the depths of despair."

—**John Watkin**, Multiple Emmy Winning Producer/Director

"I've known James Arthur Ray and have called him a friend for 13 years. I've seen the adversity he has faced, and I've witnessed how he has handled it and risen from crisis that would have made an ordinary man disappear. In the troubled times we live in, we need leaders who understand the importance of Redemption. We need leaders who have faced adversity and have risen from its ashes. James Arthur Ray has the qualities and life experiences to share and he can help us all live better more fulfilling and promising lives."

—**John Ferriter**, Chairman & CEO of the Alternative, former EVP Worldwide Head of Non-Scripted Television, The William Morris Agency

"A new, well founded definition of 'rock bottom' and 'leadership' and what you'll need to become a true leader in a world of wanna-bees. I strongly suggest you have a highlighter at your side as you read this book, don't skip-over any pages and most importantly… take action on what you'll be learning."

—**Anthony Parinello**, *Wall Street Journal*, best-selling author of *Think and Sell Like A CEO*

"In *The Business of Redemption*, James Arthur Ray's personal stories are riveting and his lessons learned are deep. No one is better equipped than James to show you exactly how to get knocked down, get back up, and come back strong. This book is a strong jolt of reality regarding what it takes to be a true leader in today's world."

—**Dr. Tony Alessandra**, author of
*The NEW Art of Managing People* and *The Platinum Rule*

"True leadership only comes from learning from our mistakes and failures. With self-reflection and an ownership of our mistakes we become greater human beings and have more to offer others. James has truly grown beyond himself into the kind of leader necessary in this new age."

—**Zen Master D. Genpo Merzel**

"In this book, James handles the disastrous circumstances which devastated many lives, including his. With honesty and in detail. He takes full responsibility for what had happened, He meant well, he meant to do good and it all went horribly wrong. Whilst reading this book I thought of all the past good deeds I had done to serve others which had not turned out as expected. I couldn't help but think that this could easily have happened me. *Redemption* took me through an emotional roller coaster ride of empathy, sadness and above all deep lessons learned of the human experience, psyche and behavior. A must read."

—**Dariush Soudi**, Chairman of The Beunique Group of Companies Dubai

"*Redemption* shares a story of tragedy along with profound—and important—lessons for leadership and life that we all can learn from."

—**Robin Sharma**, #1 bestselling author of *The Monk Who Sold His Ferrari*

"This powerful, insightful book helps you bring out of yourself strengths that you may not have known. It can change your life—sooner than you may expect."

—**Brian Tracy**, author of *Maximum Achievement*

# THE
# BUSINESS OF
# REDEMPTION

## THE PRICE OF LEADERSHIP
## IN BOTH LIFE AND BUSINESS

*NEW YORK TIMES* BESTSELLING AUTHOR

# JAMES ARTHUR RAY

NEW YORK

LONDON • NASHVILLE • MELBOURNE • VANCOUVER

# THE BUSINESS OF REDEMPTION
## THE PRICE OF LEADERSHIP IN BOTH LIFE AND BUSINESS

© 2020 James Arthur Ray

Published in New York, New York, by Morgan James Publishing. Morgan James is a trademark of Morgan James, LLC. www.MorganJamesPublishing.com

ISBN 978-1-64279-479-3  paperback
ISBN 978-1-64279-480-9  eBook
ISBN 978-1-64279-481-6  hardcover
Library of Congress Control Number: 2019933435

Morgan James is a proud partner of Habitat for Humanity Peninsula and Greater Williamsburg. Partners in building since 2006.

Get involved today! Visit
www.MorganJamesBuilds.com

# TABLE OF CONTENTS

# ACKNOWLEDGMENTS

This book has been a ten-year journey and labor of love. It has gone through so many writes and rewrites that I've lost count. So many people have contributed, written, read, and given their input. We all deeply desired to get this book right.

There are so many individuals for whom I'm eternally grateful. So many who have taught me valuable lessons throughout my life. Sometimes even when it was their objective to take me down, attack, or persecute. I've learned and grown immensely through the pain, the suffering, and the loss of the self-image I had built.

So, to all the individuals who hated and attacked . . . I honor and appreciate you. For it's through your lessons that I've become clearer, more self-confident, and more self-aware, beyond the opinions of others. I honor you and thank you, and only wish you love and peace.

I'm most indebted and grateful to those who stood with me through the perfect storm—and in many cases got knocked around by part of my storm in addition to their own. We live in interesting times to say the least.

It's easy to call yourself a "friend" when your so-called friend is on top and everyone, including the media, appears to love him. It's a completely different situation when your "friend" hits rock bottom.

It's in these moments that the acquaintances and the fair-weather are separated from the true. While I may unfortunately miss some individuals, the following are the ones who reached out, stood out, and stood strong during the storm.

Bersabeh (Bear) Ray. You are my rock, and while we had not yet found each other during the initial crisis, you have continually been there to pick me back up and help put my shattered pieces back together through the arduous comeback and climb.

You believed in me and encouraged me, even when it was hard for me to believe in myself anymore. You stood steadfast and strong when I was shattered and broken, and you helped me glue back together my suffering spirit and soul. I love and appreciate you more than any words can express. The magnificent cover design you created for this book captures the essence of its contents perfectly. You have taught me the lesson of authentic love, and a piece of you is forever in my heart and in all those I am blessed to serve. I'm beyond blessed to have you in my life and to call you my best friend, my partner, and my wife.

Jon and Cynthia Ray. Jon, you're the most steadfast, strong, and loyal brother any man could ask for. You became the "big brother" during the tsunami, and I appreciate you always listening and understanding. I deeply appreciate your compassion and strength as well. Cynthia, thank you for always being there for both me and Jon. I'm extremely blessed to have you both in my life.

Gordon and Joyce Ray (aka Dad and Mom). No words do justice. Thank you for taking the hits, barbs, and knockdowns with me. I know it hurt you deeply to see your son go through his own dark night in the public eye, and to constantly ask why. I honor you and thank you deeply. Mom, you anguished and cried with me many nights over the loss of my clients and friends, my life's work, and the loss of our innocence in so many ways. You did your very best to understand what I was going through, and it rattled your world model when the media (that you had always believed in) only desired to sensationalize and demonize. Dad, thank you as well, and I only wish that you were still here to see this book finally published. May you rest in peace, Dad; I love you both profoundly.

John Ferriter. John, you're a dear friend, and one of the very few who stood with me through the fire. You always believed in me. Even when threatened by haters yourself, even when some attempted to get you fired from your job for supporting me, you stood strong in your belief in me and my work. You're a rare breed. I love you dearly and appreciate you immensely. May you rest in peace my dear friend. The depth of your friendship and love is in this book as well.

Gail Kingsbury. Gail, you're a gem. You've been a close friend and supporter since I was just a dreamer attempting to break into the speaking industry. We've been through many starts, stops, setbacks, failures, and successes together. Thank you for your friendship. Thanks so very much for your continued belief in me and my work. Thank you for all the help and support you have given and continue to give. We've had numerous challenges to overcome in getting this book out to the world, and we're finally here. I love and appreciate you dearly.

Paige Stover-Hague. Your legal background coupled with your writing skills and hunger for this project gave me, Anne, and Angie the foundation from which to build. May you rest in peace, dear Paige, and may this book be a testament to your passion.

Anne Heliker. Thank you so much for getting the essence of me and the message that needs to be conveyed. Your organization of the material laid the foundation for what this book has eventually become.

Angie Kiesling. As you know, I've never written a book previously that had any type of plot, flow, or storyline. Performance and business books don't necessitate those qualities. Your masterful finishing touches bring the story to life, and I'm forever grateful.

Finally, and importantly: to James Shore, Liz Newman, and Kirby Brown. You honored me by being my clients and friends, and whatever I may have taught you as your advisor and coach, you have facilitated my greatest life lessons and teachings. I honor you. This book is an homage to you, your courage, and your commitment to your own life leadership and self-awareness.

## INTRODUCTION

# I AM RESPONSIBLE

I am responsible for the deaths of three people.

This reality is the complete antithesis of everything I've lived my life for or would have wished for those I'm blessed to work with. It hurts, and it hurts deeply—every single day.

On October 8, 2009, I led a Spiritual Warrior retreat in Sedona, Arizona. Nestled among the famous Red Rocks and steeped in spiritual tradition, Sedona is a natural draw for truth-seekers and others looking to push past their boundaries, those things that are holding them back. This retreat would give participants the opportunity to push the limits of their own physical, mental, emotional, and spiritual boundaries through a weeklong experience consisting of numerous introspective exercises and contemplations of unhealed trauma and unresolved emotional issues. It was tough. Emotional and yet very rewarding. The week culminated in a multiple-round sweat lodge event. The opportunity to reconnect with their inner mental toughness and emotional strength.

At my urging, three people—James Shore, Liz Newman, and Kirby Brown—pushed themselves too far, ending their lives and forever changing mine.

It was my event. My team. My sweat lodge. My choice to facilitate a dangerous exercise.

As the leader, I alone am responsible.

I didn't realize that something was horribly wrong during the sweat lodge exercise. No one did. God, how I wish I had. It wasn't apparent to me until after the exercise was over. Had I known that something was going wrong, I would have stopped. Immediately. I would have pulled up the sides of the tent and opened the door flap.

One of the sweat lodge participants was a physician, Dr. Jeanne Armstrong, MD. She was seated near James Shore and Kirby Brown in the back of the lodge. Dr. Jeanne testified under oath that she also didn't know anything was seriously wrong until everyone exited the lodge. She had no idea a life-or-death situation was occurring right next to her.

Dr. Jeanne also testified that if she had known, she would have been bound by the Hippocratic Oath to take action and help them. But even she, with her extensive medical training and experience, was unaware of the gravity of the situation.

This weighs heavily on me—more than words can convey. Bearing responsibility for a tragedy that resulted from an exercise I led is the price I must pay for the rest of my life.

## Absolute Responsibility

Let me state very clearly: no matter how much it hurts, no matter how much anguish I have over what occurred, I know it pales in comparison to the pain that family, friends, and loved ones of James, Liz, and Kirby must feel. My heart goes out to them daily, and in no way do I compare my pain to theirs.

The ultimate price of leadership is *absolute responsibility*. Absolute ownership. Of everything. For everything. No exceptions. As leaders we must take responsibility for ourselves, our choices, those we are leading, and the mistakes we may ultimately make.

Shifting responsibility onto another is never an option. I had a team that assisted with the sweat lodge exercise. Each person had a job, was highly skilled, well paid, and knew exactly what their role was. Yes, I had a team, but I was their leader. Absolute responsibility was mine. You've heard it said, and it bears repeating: the buck stops here.

It never occurred to me before, during, or after the exercise and tragic aftermath to hold anyone on my team responsible for the events that unfolded that fateful night. A true leader never throws his team under the bus.

This is the price of leadership, and if you can't step up to this, then you should just stand down. Authentic leadership will cost you something.

## One Fateful Evening

How I wish I could take back the events of October 8, 2009.

Stepping from the sweat lodge, several people were victorious, whooping out their "I did it!" proclamations. But it quickly became clear that others, many others, were not doing well at all.

As more participants came out of the lodge and their bodies reacted in the cold night air, the scene became chaotic. People were throwing up, moaning, and asking for help. Some were shaking and unable to walk.

Slowly, it dawned on me that more people than usual were in distress. Several were unconscious, foaming at the mouth, and not responding to efforts by team members to revive them.

I had *never* in all my years of holding sweat lodge events seen *anyone* foam at the mouth. *This is crazy. What's going on?*

A big commotion erupted on the back side of the lodge. I walked around to the back and saw Kirby Brown and James Shore lying on the ground. Their color was wrong. Very wrong. They were bluish and their lips were pale.

Someone said, "They're not breathing."

These words echoed in my mind and hung like a heavy anchor in the air.

Within the hour, as police and emergency vehicles swarmed the area, I would hear a detective say, "Mr. Ray, I hope you know we're investigating this as a homicide."

Everything went silent. I glanced over at the sweat lodge; they had already roped off the area with yellow crime scene tape.

*A homicide?*

"Look, you might go to jail tonight," a criminal lawyer told me later that evening. "If you do, we'll get you out as soon as we can."

*Jail? Are you kidding me?* My head was spinning fast, and I thought I just might throw up.

## CHAPTER 1

# 267823—The New Fish

My "fall" wasn't terminal, but it *was* catastrophic. I thought I had lost everything: my business, my life savings, my reputation, and my home.

I would quickly realize, however, that I had lost even more.

I went from a privileged life on Mulholland Drive in Beverly Hills to "the hole." Solitary confinement. Right next to death row. My own personal descent into hell.

As we drove through the Arizona night, a thousand stars twinkling overhead, I was shackled at my waist and ankles and chained to the seat. The men shackled next to me spoke a language I didn't understand; I wasn't sure I even *wanted* to understand. Their breath and bodies smelled like anger, stale coffee, cigarettes, and death.

When we picked up the guys from maximum security, they filed to the van with a waddle that was fast becoming familiar: the waddle of legs shackled just inches apart. The guy next to me said through three brown, cracked teeth, "These motherf***** haven't seen sunlight in years."

As they crammed into the van and shoved up next to me, their ghostly white skin confirmed that my new colleague wasn't lying.

I had no idea where I was going.

I wasn't sure I wanted to know.

I was scared to death.

Everything I knew about prison I'd learned from watching HBO. And what I knew wasn't pretty. What I learned on the bus that night was that I didn't want to be "ventilated" (stabbed), raped by one of the "Cheetos" (gay men), or beaten to a pulp by any of the guys shackled around me, who spent way too much time bragging about their conquests and beatings.

As the shoulder-to-shoulder-packed van rambled down the highway, their tales were legion. Each story was more brutal and frightening than the last. Suddenly I was Alice, cast into a surreal underworld peopled by strange characters where nothing made sense. I was spinning quickly down a *very* dark rabbit hole.

*How did I get here?*

We drove all night and arrived at a prison facility known as The Walls that housed death row. My new "home" was right next door to the most hardened of criminals, criminals whose lives would soon end. They were sentenced to give their lives for whatever they had given their lives for.

---

**We all give our lives for something.**

---

I would come to know from experience, and future conversations, that these guys gave their lives for something much less than they would have wished. Potential and purpose were wasted on impulse and lack of emotional discipline and mastery.

### Falling into the "Why Me?" Mentality

Barely morning, a mist covering the ground, and I could just make out two 25-foot walls lined with coils of barbed wire on the top. An even taller fence stood between them with more barbed wire.

I shuffled across the yard, working on the mandatory waddle, with my ankles and hands still tightly shackled. I passed cages with guys in them, curious guys, angry guys. I could almost see and feel the inner animal in each of them—and I would soon hear it.

I glanced at the 25-foot wall to my left and the caged men to my right. Then I stared at the gravel beneath my feet as I shuffled along: *crunch, crunch, jangle, crunch.* Taking full steps wasn't an option—not even close.

The crunching of the gravel and scraping of the chains took me into my own internal world like a trance, my only means of escape. I focused on the dust covering my orange pant legs and realized: *I'm going nowhere. I may never make it out alive.*

This realization was the start of what would become my "why me" mentality. We've all been there. When things aren't going our way, when tragedy or crisis enters our lives, it's almost human nature to ask, "Why me?" Have you ever done this?

The problem is, when we adopt this mentality and ask this question once or multiple times, we spiral deeper and deeper into our own personal hell. I was quickly spiraling into the pit.

We all have our own personal hell, and sometimes life brings us more than one. When that happens, we can't ask why. Asking why unleashes the mighty victim archetype—mighty only in its ability to completely ruin and destroy our lives. To leave us like a helpless little puddle of ailments in our own self-pity.

Victims are unable to see the light or come up with an exit strategy. They have no resilience or resourcefulness. If we spend too much of our energy wondering why me, why now, and, well, just *why*, we won't have the energy or the ability to learn.

Look, we all take hits. Not one of us is immune. The biggest difference between the victim and the victor is how long we spend feeling sorry for ourselves. Period.

I'm not suggesting we'll never feel like a victim. We will. I certainly did. But the sooner we move in a new direction, the sooner we will live again, regardless of circumstances.

---

*Leaders who play victim lose their ability to lead.*

---

This is absolute responsibility, and it will absolutely change your life.

It's *not* about circumstances. It's about how you choose to experience and *use* circumstances.

Our best lessons in life will come from our tragedies, our crises, our mistakes, and, yes, our own personal hell. We have to embrace these opportunities and emerge from a painful situation armed with even more inner strength, more emotional and mental mastery, and more knowledge—and hopefully wisdom—than we ever had before.

I already knew this when I arrived at The Walls. But when my uncertainties and unknowns became frightening realities, I did start to think, *Why me?*

## Learning to Accept My "New Role"

I had been transferred to The Walls from Alhambra, and I remembered a carving on the bunk above me there that said exactly what I was thinking at that moment: "I have natural life plus five. Basically I'm f*****."

I was f*****.

I couldn't imagine the feeling of a "life plus five" sentence, but that last part resonated through my head and gut fully and completely.

When I was being escorted out of Alhambra on the way to The Walls, one of the guards pulled me aside and said, "Look, Ray. Where you're going, don't trust anyone. They will act like they're your friends. They're not your friends. They'll rob you, extort you, and stab you faster than you can blink an eye. Don't trust anyone. Just do your time, lay low, get home, and get on with your life."

Not very comforting, to say the least. But his words were spot-on truth about what was to come.

Yes. I was f*****. My thoughts rampaged like a wild boar on steroids.

All the guys knew immediately who I was. The media had done its job well. So the games began: "Hey, sweat lodge guru! What's up, motherf*****? We're gonna f*** you up! What'd you do, motherf*****? Lock them in and fry their asses? Hey, guru, can you save me? You look kinda pretty. You're going to be *really* popular in here, big boy."

The laughter and banter sent chills up my spine. The bonfire of fear was raging and growing inside me. So were thoughts of being stabbed, raped, or getting the living hell beat out of me. I was about to go into mental meltdown.

I knew I had to grab onto a new strategy fast or I was going to lose it. I got resourceful. Functional? That's debatable. Denial can be deadly at worst and dysfunctional at best. But sometimes you grab onto whatever lifeline you can find.

I said to myself, "Alright, James, man, you've got to get your head on."

Then it dawned on me: I'm a method actor. I've played a lot of roles in my life: Salesman. Transformational speaker. Bestselling author. Coach. Businessman. Entrepreneur. TV personality.

Convict.

I was now a convict, and I had to do exactly what I'd done for my more desirable roles. Study. Do the research. Immerse myself in the role. Be the best damn convict I could ever be.

At some level, we all pretend. We keep our darkness hidden from the light of others and stuffed in the basement. Pretending in prison is even harder than pretending in real life. It helped for about a week. In prison, just as in life and leadership, you fail miserably being anything other than your true self.

Until you're sitting in a cell, little do you realize how few circumstances in life force you to be completely real and brutally honest with yourself. Living in an 8-by-10 cell certainly forces you to do that.

I was taken to cellblock 5 (CB 5). The building reminded me of an octopus with a large tower in the center. The tower was filled with guards and guns—big guards and big guns. The legs of the octopus reached out from the central tower. That's how the guards kept watch down each corridor.

An armed guard with a walkie-talkie escorted me from the gravel yard into the building. We stopped outside a large door.

"Open CB 5," the guard barked into his walkie. The heavy steel door slid open.

"New fish."

As we stepped across the threshold, I could see movement in the cells that lined the walls both left and right. Faces were pressed against tiny rectangular windows, just large enough to expose one eye, staring out at me, watching me, from behind the cell doors.

As I shuffled past each door, I heard, "New fish."

The anger and bitterness from those eyes, one after the other, pierced me like a knife. The feeling sent a cold chill up my spine. Finally, we stopped outside a door on the left wall.

"Open number seven," the guard barked again.

My mind flashed to my studies of numerology. I had always been a voracious student of many things from business to mysticism. In numerology, my Life Path number is a seven. Was it a sign? Was it symbolic? Was God sending me a message? I was desperately searching for meaning, trying to make sense of the senseless.

Another large steel door slowly slid open, and I looked inside. The tiny space was filthy, reeking of urine and excrement. The small steel toilet, sink, and faucet were caked with calcium. My new bed was a concrete slab with a urine-stained mattress, maybe an inch thick at best. No pillow. Cold concrete walls and floor.

*This is it*, I thought. *Two years in this cold, filthy place.*

I shuffled in, and the putrid piss smell overwhelmed me. I knew that smell. I flashed back to the very first studio apartment I rented in Tulsa, Oklahoma, during college. The previous owner's cat had evidently decided to relieve itself all over the carpet and walls. In that part of town, thorough cleanup and repair were not part of the deal. However, compared to what I was looking at, that apartment was a *palace*. I would've given everything to be back there right then.

---

*Funny the things we take for granted. Funny how self-importance leaches the gratitude for what we have right out of our fingers.*

---

"Close cell seven." The door banged shut behind me.

*I'm still cuffed*, I thought. I figured the guard had forgotten and I would be like this for God only knew how long. But he didn't forget; this was procedure.

"Back up, inmate," he said. Inmate. *How the hell did this happen?* Instantly I was transformed from a human being to a thing.

I backed up to a small trap door at waist height in the middle of my door and held out my wrists. He reached in, undid the cuffs, and pulled them back out. And that's where I stayed for the better part of the next month.

In solitary confinement.

No TV. No radio. No books. No pen or paper. Nothing.

## Solitary Loneliness

When I arrived, I thought this was my final destination. I thought this was where I would be staying my entire sentence. All I could do was assume because no one told me anything. I was "property of the state," so I was informed of nothing, not even about my own life. Property has no life and therefore doesn't need to know.

It was just me and the walls. The profanity-filled banter of the other prisoners streaming through the air vents was relentless. Angry men, full of hate and bitterness and uncomfortable with their own loneliness and silence, did everything possible to escape their fate.

I was only allowed out of my cell twice a week when, still in shackles, I was put into a cage on the yard for forty-five minutes. Here, this was considered recreation.

Twice a week, I was also escorted, in handcuffs, to a shower. The showers were also in a very small cage. We showered in front of guards—male and female.

Every time I exited my cell for a shower, for rec, for any reason, I was strip-searched, including all cavities. This was an indignity I never expected to experience. I wouldn't wish it upon my worst enemy.

Then it was back into cuffs and back to the cell. In the cell it was just me and God—and Kirby, and James, and Liz.

## Meeting Eddie

When I was in solitary, I literally had no contact with any other inmate. Then one day I met Eddie.

Eddie was a porter who had natural life, plus five. Initially, this made no sense to me, but I later learned it meant he had zero chance of ever getting out of this place. This was maximum security. Right next door to death row. Only the most hardened and dangerous offenders were housed here.

Eddie would later teach me that the system added this "life plus" factor so that in the extreme long shot he may ever come up for parole, he would still have another sentence to serve. He was completely despondent when he schooled me on this protocol. Basically, Eddie was going nowhere.

As he swung the mop down the long run of CB 5, he came to my cell door. I couldn't see him as he talked with me because we could only talk through the very slim crack that allowed the heavy steel door to slide on its track.

"Hey, aren't you Mr. Ray?" he said. To hear myself called "Mr." here was a strange formality I hadn't heard for a while. Like everyone else in here, Eddie already knew who I was.

"Yeah, I am."

"Hey, my name's Eddie," he said as I heard the mop continue to swish in the hall. If the guards in the pod at the end saw him stopping and talking with anyone, there would be retribution.

"How are you doing, Eddie? And how are you out of your cell?" I asked him.

"Well, I've been here so long they trust me, and I porter the hallways, clean things up," he explained. "But I can't talk long because the guards are watching, and they'll call me on it."

This was the beginning of what became daily conversations made up of sound-bites through the crack in the door.

One day Eddie asked me if I had anything to read in my cell. I didn't. I had nothing. Not even a paper and a pen. Just me. My thoughts. And God.

"Well, let me see what I can find," he said to me.

He brought me a magazine, which happened to be an Eastern mysticism magazine, a magazine on Hinduism—something I was definitely interested in. Who would have ever thought? In truth, he could have brought me pretty much anything within reason, and I would've taken it. I love to read, and yet in my endless search for meaning it seemed quite auspicious that what he brought me was a spiritual text. My spirit longed to make meaning out of the seemingly meaningless. I had contemplated my life and circumstances ad nauseum while staring at four graffiti-filled walls, day in and day out.

Eddie and I struck up a relationship, and our brief, through-the-door conversations became almost a daily ritual. One day he disclosed to me that he was in for murder. He was beyond remorseful.

Some time and many brief conversations passed, and once again Eddie was at my door. "Hey, do you drink coffee?" he asked.

At the time, I didn't. I had given it up completely several years before I went to prison.

I thought to myself, *What the hell? I'm stuck in here. I may as well.*

"Sure, I'll drink some coffee," I said.

When Eddie returned, he shoved a little baggie of instant coffee through the gap in the door. "Put this in your water bottle," he instructed.

They issued prisoners water bottles because the cells had no water fountain. I had to fill the water bottle with water from the nasty, calcium-crusted sink. I've always been somewhat of a water snob, optioning for only the most alkaline and filtered options. Not here. Acid and calcium and chemicals were my only option to stay hydrated.

He then shoved an absolute abomination through the door. It was a contraption that literally consisted of two bare wires attached to a long cord with a plug on the other end. Several clusters of jerry-rigged tape were holding this horror together.

"Plug that in and put it in your water bottle," he told me.

All I could think was, *Yeah, right! Are you kidding me? I'm gonna get electrocuted and die in this cell!*

"Eddie, man, this thing looks scary."

"Don't worry," he assured me. "It'll be okay."

*James, this is a man who has already admitted to three murders. With so many who have a bone to pick with you, do you really trust this?*

My mind flashed back to a threatening note I found on my dinner tray in the county jail. My paranoia was running rampant. Or was it just wisdom?

*Okay, what the hell.* I plugged it in, dropped it in the water bottle, and jumped back as far as I could. Almost instantly the water boiled. I later learned that what Eddie had given me was called a "stinger," which you can actually buy at camping stores. I would later buy one from the commissary, just a little more sophisticated and safer than what I was working with.

I started drinking this rancid coffee and instantly got a caffeine buzz. I couldn't remember the last time I'd had a cup of coffee. Probably a decade or more, and this was nasty. As I sat on my bunk, starting to buzz, I thought, *Damn, this is kind of nice. This is a good day!*

Interesting how when you have nothing except what you need to keep you alive, even the smallest of luxuries—in this case, a cup of barely drinkable coffee—can make your entire day.

"I really f***** up," Eddie said to me one day. "I can't take it back, and I can't fix it. But, James, I got kids, and I'm never gonna see them again. They can't even come visit me. Sometimes I just don't know how I can do this."

"Eddie," I said, "let me tell you a story."

I was smashed against the iron door, doing my best to convey a story that I prayed would have impact.

"Do you know who Gandhi is, Eddie?"

"Yeah, I think I've heard of him."

I explained how Gandhi wanted liberation for his people in India. They practiced passive resistance to make a point. At one point, all his people were starving, including Gandhi. They had no food, and it was a very difficult time. One day, a reporter said to Gandhi, "Bapu," which means *father* or *teacher* in Sanskrit, "you're standing here just skin and bones; all your people are as well. How is it that you're so happy and all the rest of your people are suffering and starving?" Gandhi responded, "Because I'm not starving; I'm choosing to fast."

I paused then asked, "Do you get it, Eddie?"

"Well, kind of," he replied.

I continued. "Here's the thing. Gandhi was in physical pain. He was hungry. Everyone was hungry. But he used his mind to choose his misery, to embrace the situation he was in and do it willfully. By choice."

I let that sink in for a few seconds and then said, "Eddie, you're not getting out of here. You know that. So you can be miserable and suffer for the rest of your days, or you can choose it."

"Hmmm," he said. "Okay, I gotta go." And he was off with his mop.

Nothing more was said about that conversation for the rest of the time I was in solitary.

Late one night, a guard came to my cell and told me I was rolling out at four o'clock the next morning. Of course, they didn't tell me where I was going, but I would later find out I was being transferred to minimum security, Eagle Point.

They pulled me out of my cell and had me spread-eagle up against a wall when I heard a voice from the other end of the run.

"Mr. Ray! Mr. Ray!" It was Eddie. I turned my head in the direction of his voice.

"Eyes forward, inmate!" the guard barked.

"Yeah," I shouted back as I snapped my eyes to the wall.

"It's Eddie, good luck, man. And just so you know—I'm choosing it."

Even though I was surrounded by hardened guards, I couldn't control my emotions. Eddie was my first and only human contact during my time in solitary. In different ways, we looked out for and helped each other.

Though I never saw Eddie again, and never will, I won't ever forget the short-lived connection we formed. And I'm forever grateful that he helped me by allowing me to help him.

Eddie was a good man at heart. He just didn't have the right resources to actualize his goodness fully. I know, deep down in my soul, that we all do the best we can with the resources we have available. People are basically good. All of them. They just choose poor strategies and behaviors due to limited resources.

Our opportunity as leaders is to have the understanding, maybe compassion, not to label people as their behaviors. That's not who they are. Not really. People choose to behave, but they're not their behavior.

Given greater opportunity, learning, and resources, they may choose different strategies. When you understand a person, you don't have to agree. Understanding and agreement are not the same thing.

You can strongly disagree with someone's behavior, like I did with Eddie and the behavior he chose that landed him in for life, but at the same time still have compassion and understanding for the person.

Though it's a great leadership reminder, it applies to all relationships—both personal and professional. Thanks, Eddie.

## Lessons from Eagle Point

I was finally on a bus, headed to Eagle Point, the minimum-security prison where I would do the bulk of my time: two years that would feel more like twenty. At first I felt a great sense of relief as I left The Walls, but that didn't last long.

Eagle Point. I was still looking for meaning, and I found it in that name. As a child, I had been fascinated by eagles. As an adult, I had paintings of them in my various offices, carvings of them in stone, and statues in my hallways. This memory seemed comforting as I grabbed at straws. Eagle Point. It seemed appropriate—maybe even destiny.

The first thing I saw as the van arrived was a sea of guys in orange on the yard, and my romantic idealism and sense of semi-comfort waned. My mind returned to the myriad stories of rapes, beatings, and ventilations I had heard on the other van ride.

I thought, *Oh my God, I have to walk out there? Into that deadly sea of orange?*

You see, up to that point, I hadn't interacted in any free space with another inmate. I had been in solitary for weeks. I showered alone, save for the ever-present gaze of the guard outside the locked steel cage. I was inside a locked cage when outside on rec. I was safe, always alone. I didn't know what would happen out there with the other prisoners. I see a poignant life lesson here as we all build our own walls of self-limitation and boundaries.

---

*Our barriers of confinement can quickly become our fields of comfort.*

---

With no walls or cages to protect me, I shuddered as my wild-boar imagination went into overdrive once again.

In a weird way, solitary confinement comforted and consoled me. I had been a loner all my life, an extreme introvert. I was fond of taking vacations alone all over the world, just sitting with myself and contemplating life.

This had been misinterpreted many times by those who knew me as a public figure. When I was onstage, I came alive and was extremely animated. In the flow state of stage, I was very different from my quiet, contemplative, and introverted offstage persona. A client once said to me, "James, when you're onstage, it's as if the entire universe comes through you. When you're offstage, it's as if you're empty."

Offstage, I was much more comfortable in my own company or in the company of great books and great minds. I had always been my own best friend. This contrast caused many to label me as aloof or unapproachable. Little did they know I had only one date my entire time in high school because I was too introverted and insecure to ask a young lady out. I just knew, no matter who she was, the answer would be no. So I chose to live in my quiet inner world and avoid the risk.

But how was I going to find solitude and solace in this orange sea? Before me was the greatest risk I could imagine. Fear pulsed through me. Maybe solitary confinement wasn't so bad after all. A heavy metal door gave a sense of security.

We all build walls. In our minds, they protect us and keep us from harm and emotional hurt. But they create the very thing we so desperately want to avoid— shutting us off from other human beings.

My arrival was a circus, and that first day I was the main attraction: "Step right up, gentleman, and see the man who was once famous and fabulous! The man who went from media star to media Satan in the blink of an eye. The man who was once confident and had all the answers for both life and business. Now he doesn't have answers for shit. See him in his new shattered and insecure state. The man who once seemed to be on top of the world!"

Like before, they all knew me already and jeered as I walked past. Same song, second verse. But this time these guys could walk right up to me—at least as close as the guard allowed.

"Can I have your autograph, guru?"

"You gotta motivate me, man."

"Hey, you wanna do a sweat lodge, motherf*****?"

They all laughed as they tried to one-up each other with their jokes and banter.

As the guard escorted me down the sidewalk, I looked ahead and saw what appeared to be a woman. Tall and slender, with long black hair cascading down her back, her hips were swaying from side to side. Yet she was in the same orange clothes I was in.

I turned to the guard and asked, "You have women here?"

He smirked. "We have some men who *think* they're women."

This guy had it down, and he was working it. He sure had me fooled. I would later learn his self-appointed name, his handle, was Angel. Angel and I had some interesting conversations before his release. I eventually became the go-to guy for many before they exited. But I'm getting ahead of myself.

The rules here were new. You had to be in your cell for a head count at eleven in the morning, four in the afternoon, and eleven at night. Otherwise, you could roam the yard as you wished, visit the library, play an instrument in the band room, shoot basketball, or do whatever you wanted within the confines of the prison. Just like a one-star resort, right? Wrong. On the surface, it all seemed pretty nice compared to death row. But surface appearances are deceiving.

> *External worlds tell vastly different stories than the internal darkness residing just below the surface.*

The first of the four different cellmates I had was an ex-cop from Arizona named Jimmy, who seemed friendly and helpful. Jimmy was in for drug charges. I would later learn that most of the former police officers here were in on drug charges. I found it interesting that supposed enforcers of the law were some of the greatest offenders. But, then again, I'd seen the fiasco of a court system we have, so this was just one more brick in the dysfunctional wall.

At first I was relieved to have a former officer as a cellmate, a "cellie" as the inmates would call him. But Jimmy ended up stealing from me. Calling prison a "reform system" is a joke. No reform is happening inside, just plain punishment and degradation. The 85 percent recidivism rate is no surprise. Prison is big business, with financials and budgets involved. Property of the state is big money and big business.

## Getting Real

Eagle Point was where I first sat down and looked at my life and situation clearly, exactly as it was. No positive spin, no Jedi mind tricks, no reframing, no "what can I learn from this?" It just plain sucked. Yet I embraced it. I let deep despair, anguish, and helplessness hit me like a big black truck. I reached the height of my *why me?* mentality.

Up until then, I was playing games. Method acting. Avoiding and suppressing. I remember sitting in the back office of the courtroom after they had taken me into custody, after four months of hearing the prosecutor bastardize my teachings and philosophies, twisting them, taking them completely out of context. I remember telling myself that I would show them all. I would make a difference when I got to prison. I told myself I would make a positive impact on those guys.

I found something very different waiting for me, something much less romantic and idealistic. Most of these guys couldn't care less that people once paid me ten grand a pop to hear what *they* could potentially hear for free. They didn't give two shakes about what I had to say. They were so drunk on their own wine they didn't care that I could potentially offer them finer wine. None but a very, very few, that is.

Of course, the big reveal was that I was drunk on my own wine as well. Sloppy drunk.

Why did I go into leadership and personal performance to begin with? Without a doubt, first and foremost, it was to develop and save myself. Growing up as an insignificant, introverted, and insecure wallflower left lots of room where self-love and acceptance should have gone.

Then again, maybe it was because it made me feel significant to be the guy making a difference in people's lives and businesses, the guy helping others save themselves from their own self-inflicted misery and self-imposed limitations.

I quickly realized that, in this place, I had to get good at just trying to save myself once again, trying to make a difference in me. Hopefully I could do this at much deeper and more honest levels than ever before. I wasn't here to lead others. I was here to lead myself and win the war within.

Authentic and powerful leadership of others *only* comes, when and if it does, when you first powerfully lead your own life; when you take absolute responsibility for who you are and *why* you are; when you own your self-limitation, self-doubt, self-importance, and, frankly, your downright nonsense and complete bullshit.

I didn't socialize. This was easy for me. Like I said, I had always been my own best friend. I'm not anti-social but rather quite *non*-social. I always have been and probably always will be. True self-awareness will never be found in a social setting, not at a deep level anyway.

*Deep self-awareness and potential greatness always seek solitude.*

Even a brief study of the greatest leaders and world-changers throughout history will quickly prove this true. But it's rarely understood. Non-social beings in a world of socialites are often grossly misunderstood.

Things were no different here.

### The Reality of Escape

One day, Pisas, one of the Hispanic gang leaders at Eagle Point, came to my cell door as I read on my bunk and asked, "Why don't you like these guys?"

"I don't not like these guys," I responded.

"Then why don't you ever come out and watch TV with us?"

"I don't really watch TV," I explained.

"I'll make them watch what you want to watch," he responded.

"I appreciate that," I told him, "but I really just prefer to read."

He scowled at me, not buying it. He thought for sure I didn't like them because hanging out in front of the TV and laughing was what *everyone* does, right?

Not me.

I tried to make the most of my time by lying on my bunk and reading for ten to fourteen hours per day. But I soon realized that this was merely my escape. The way other guys here used drugs or sex or working out or sitting in front of the TV, I used books and journaling. Once I recognized my own escapism, I forced myself to just *be* with what was, which was sheer anguish, disillusionment, and pain.

Jumping ahead, I found that anything you look at clearly, squarely, and head-on eventually disappears. What you resist tends to persist. The more you run from a problem or a lie, the faster it chases and the harder it haunts you.

Gradually, I just stopped running and said, *Alright. This sucks. This hurts. But today, instead of letting it crush me, I'm going to be courageous enough just to be with my own pain.* You see, the reality is, running from pain is painful. Or if not painful, depressing.

While this may seem counterintuitive, it takes tremendous courage to allow fear to exist without running, hiding, or avoiding. Running from fear is fearful. So I just sat with it. I tried to understand it, to feel it, and to learn from being with it instead of applying a self-help bandage or "positive" spin.

---

*True positive thinking is not expecting the best. That's illusion. Positive thinking is accepting that what is happening is the best for your own development and growth.*

---

While facing fear seems so logical, it's not always easy to do in "real life." We all have fears, but how much time do we spend looking into ourselves and truly getting in touch with those fears?

True leaders must see things exactly as they are. Not better. Not worse. Just exactly as they are. Only when you see things this clearly are you empowered to do anything to change or improve.

**Magnificent Obsession**

I was reminded of the story of the Spartan battle of Thermopylae that I love so much. Three hundred Spartan warriors held off what scholars believe to be between one hundred thousand to one hundred and fifty thousand Persian warriors for two full days.

Prior to Thermopylae, the Spartan warrior King Leonidas told his soldiers, "Ready your breakfast and eat hearty, for tonight we dine in hell!"

This is leadership that sees and communicates clearly: It won't be pretty. It won't be easy. You may not make it. But let's get the job done.

You might say my salvation came at some level from seeing things very clearly, and this came from sitting in my own pain: It's not pretty. It won't be easy. You may not make it. But let's get the job done.

My mind raced and spun:

*My God . . . how could this be real? I lost three friends.*

*God . . . if you really exist, which I now doubt you do, you would know how much I've anguished over the loss of my friends. You'd know my heart and how much I cared for them. You'd know how every single day, almost every single moment, nonstop, I've asked myself what I missed. Could I have done something differently?*

*My heart is damaged. My soul is plagued. Is that not enough? How the hell could my life have come to this? How could this be my reward? Damn you, God! Damn you! And I don't even care if I go to hell for saying that. You can't scare me with your bullshit. Hell? I'm already in hell!*

*How could it be any worse? I've lost everything. I lost my friends, my home, my life savings, my business . . . It took me twenty long years to build that business! It was my entire life! I thought it was my legacy—now it's gone! My mom has stage 4 cancer, my dad has Alzheimer's, and I'm stuck in this hellhole. I can't help them, and I may never see them again. My reputation . . . they're calling me a killer. Me! And now I'm living in a cage with common criminals.*

*My own self-importance and self-pity were in full swing. Then suddenly:*

*James, do you think you're better than they are? These so-called common criminals. Don't you think I love all humanity?*

*Damn you, God! Now you show up just to chastise me? F\*\*\* you! I can't take anymore! I don't know how I can do this!*

*James, you never get more than you can handle.*

*F\*\*\* that! And don't give me that "everything happens for a reason" bullshit either. Please!*

*James.*

*Why me?*

*Why not you, James? Do you think you're so special that only good things should happen to you?*

That stopped me like hitting a brick wall. I thought on that one, long and hard.

I asked myself: Why did you do what you did for people? Why did you travel so often and sacrifice so much to help others?

Bottom line: I realized that, ultimately, I did it for myself. It was *my* reason for being. *My* magnificent obsession. *My* purpose. Ultimately, we all do things for our own reasons.

All true leaders have a cause, and they're committed to that cause above and beyond all comfort. They feel the compelling pull of something greater than themselves. If they last, that is.

Leonidas and his three hundred were willing to give themselves fully to their cause. Even if it meant dining in hell for eternity. So if I must dine in my own hell, shouldn't I likewise be as committed?

Success is hard. Life is hard. Business is hard. So you better be doing something you love with an obsessive passion. A magnificent obsession. For if it's something of greatness, it will take every single thing you have and then some.

And, yes, as cliché as it may sound, everything *does* happen for a reason. We may find out the reason right away, or we may sometimes have to wait years. However, one thing is absolutely certain: we won't ever know *why* something happens to us if we don't look honestly and deeply for the answer.

---

**If it's true that everything happens for a reason, then the hardest thing of all is waiting for the reason and answer to appear.**

---

If we spend too much time fixated on the bad hand we've been dealt, we'll more than likely miss it when the good cards are dealt right in front of us.

I thought about Mother Teresa—the closest person to a true saint I could imagine. Why did she give so selflessly to others? Did some kind of self-interest drive her to give? She felt she was doing God's will and that had to feel good.

Isn't there some deep-seated self-interest, some congruence with our own personal values, that drives every single action in life?

Isn't it entirely possible, if not probable, that while Mother Teresa obviously cared for others, she was ultimately driven by her obsession to do God's will, which was something much bigger than herself, something worth making great sacrifices for? And in giving her all for others, did she feel good acting in congruence with her values? Did *doing* good make her *feel* good?

I have to believe the answer is yes to all of the above. Check your own experiences and see if this isn't true.

I continued my contemplation. If I did good things for others with the expectation of being rewarded and protected by life or God, was that the right reason? Certainly it wasn't.

If I did good things because it felt good, because it allowed me to live in alignment with my own personal values and purpose, then did I not, in effect, receive my payment the very *instant* I performed the action or deed?

Man, this was an awakening for me.

Isn't the same true in leadership, relationships, business, and all aspects of life? If we're doing something to get something in return, it's entirely the wrong motivation. But when we do for the sake of doing, and realize it feels congruent and good to do it, then it matters not what the return, action, or outcome may be. You get your return in the moment of action.

I had received my payment. This situation didn't impact that at all. With this realization, I felt a shift happening within me. My own self-illusion and self-importance peeled away just a bit. I saw a bit more clearly and felt a little more fully.

But the questions kept coming.

## Reasonable Doubt

I contemplated the fact that I had hired the very best doctor money could buy, Ian Paul, MD, who had a board certification in forensic pathology and was currently in the Department of Pathology in the Office of the Medical Investigator at the University of Mexico. His previous work had been conducted at Harvard University, Brown, and a host of other esteemed institutions of medicine and academia. His CV looked like the resume of a medical Superman.

Ian had pored through over four thousand pages of medical records of those who became ill during the sweat lodge, as well as the records of James, Kirby, and Liz. Dr. Paul then testified under oath that the evidence, the presenting symptoms of the individuals, proved the cause of death was *not* heat.

My making the lodge "too hot" was the state's whole argument and prosecution—even though no thermometer or measurement device of any kind was ever present in the lodge. It was all speculation—life-impacting speculation—by those who hadn't been there.

Rather, according to Dr. Paul's research, the cause of death was organophosphates—more specifically, pesticides. A quick perusal of internet articles will show how deadly pesticides can be if they enter the bloodstream, even in very small doses.

The owners of the property my company rented the lodge from, as well as the facilities where we conducted the event, initially testified that they never used pesticides on the property. One of their employees subsequently testified that the grounds were sprayed periodically, and it also came out that the tarps used for the sweat lodge tent were stored with rat poison.

Finally, the fire tender testified that they used pressed wood for the fire which is also a well-known toxic when burned. This is a well-known dangerous activity *not* ever to be done.

The owners, Michael and Amira Hamilton were perjured and called back to admit that they did indeed use pesticides on the property.

Hot bodies sitting on the bare ground where pesticides have been sprayed, with pores opened by the heat, can easily absorb the small amounts of poison that can be deadly.

Dr. Archiaus Mosley, MD, one of the state's own coroners testified under oath that he had never even been *shown* the medical records by the state, and now that he saw the records for the first time, he too believed organophosphates to be the cause of death.

Reasonable doubt. Done.

In fact, he testified that confusion on the cause of death was what caused him and the other coroners so much difficulty in coming to any conclusions. He went on to say that had he seen the records, which he hadn't, he would have *demanded* a blood sample.

All of this ping-ponged around in my mind as I sat in my own pain in prison. Ironically, I shifted from blame and victimization to complete gratitude. You see, I realized I had been in the lodge for twelve rounds, and I never once left. Yes, I was sitting by the door flap as was customary for the leader of any lodge.

Yes, that position did afford me cool and fresh air when the flap was raised as participants exited at the end of each round. Yet I was still in there the *entire* time; I never left. My body was extremely hot and obviously my pores were open. I was sitting barelegged on the dirt as well. My shirtless back was leaning against the tent tarps off and on during the event. Several people got sick, and three people lost their lives. And here I was, alive and well, albeit a bit battered and bruised.

I asked myself, *James, would you rather be sitting here in your so-called hellhole right now, as ugly and vile as it is, or would you rather be gone?*

## Choosing to Remove the Shackles

From a variety of sources, I've learned there are basically three types of incarceration: concentration camps, state prison, and federal prison. There are finer nuances, like county jail, but these are the big three, and they all vary in intensity.

Concentration camps are crucibles of human injustice and pain. Nothing can compare to this, as far as darkness goes. On the opposite side of the spectrum is federal prison. Numerous sources have compared federal prison to a three-star resort that you just can't leave. It's not a five-star resort, but it's nowhere near comparable to state prison.

In state prison, where I spent my sentence, you're an animal at worst and a number at best. "Property of the state" is what you're labeled and exactly how you're treated. Not a human being. Property. And you're reminded of this repeatedly. I was 267823. That's how I was forced to check in for meals. That was the "name" I was constantly asked to declare.

At one point, I was living in a dorm room with thirty-five angry men in 130-degree heat in the middle of the Arizona desert. No air conditioner. Guys were shooting up heroin around the clock, less than six feet away from me. In fact, the biggest drug dealer on the yard was in the bunk right next to me.

An endless procession of guys looking for their own form of escape, their fix, filed past my bunk every single day. Nothing like trying to meditate at four in the morning while hearing the *slap, slap, slap* of addicts searching desperately in the darkness for a fresh vein.

Bottom line, this was a dark and ugly place. It wasn't a concentration camp; things can always be worse. But it was no federal prison either, no three-star resort. This was *prison*.

Yet, even so, I had to admit that I wasn't yet ready to exit this life. I still believed I had work to do in the world. I was in that lodge for twelve rounds, shirtless, barelegged, and exposed, and I could just as easily be gone. But I wasn't.

As ugly and painful as this place was, I chose to be grateful to be here versus gone. And with that choice, another shift occurred. I made a decision to get over it, to get up and get on with it. Even better, to *use* this experience as an opportunity to develop, advance, and grow. And maybe, just maybe, to help others even more deeply and fully than I ever had before as a result.

I had found my own personal hell in a very literal prison, but I wasn't going to let myself stay there. I knew I had to *physically* stay, but mentally I held the keys to remove the shackles and open the doors. I could at least learn and grow. I chose leadership. I chose to lead my life fully and powerfully, even in far less than ideal circumstances.

Think of a time in your life when it seemed like nothing was going your way. You may even be there now. Life seems to be conspiring against you. Or maybe you're suffering through a huge tragedy. Maybe your business is in the tank, and you don't know how to make payroll, much less your own mortgage. Maybe your spouse just gave you shocking news or left. Maybe the doctor told you you're in physical trouble. This is your own personal hell, a theoretical prison.

We've all been there. If you haven't yet, just give it time. No one is immune. The big black truck pulls up in front of every household eventually. It isn't easy to pull ourselves out of the darkness, mentally. Far from easy. Many choose to stay in their self-inflicted prisons because they don't make the conscious choice to battle and fight their way out of it. It's always easier to be the victim, or at least it feels that way in the short-term.

We may not always have control over what happens in our lives, but we do have control over how we allow these things to impact our lives. Sometimes you just have to get over it and get on with it.

## Keep Climbing, No Matter What

I thought about the time I trekked to the top of Salcantay, the highest peak in Peru. I remembered how many times throughout that two-week journey I wanted so desperately to quit. Every fiber of my being screamed and told me I was insane to have chosen this climb. It seemed oh-so-sexy and exciting in the planning stage.

*What the hell was I thinking?*

Through pain, muscle cramps, exhaustion, and the inability to breathe, I just kept climbing. Through biting wind and frozen toes and fingers, I just kept climbing.

When I reached the summit, the rush I felt was certainly influenced by the breathtaking view. But, more important, the rush came from knowing exactly what it took to get there. If it'd been an easy uphill slope, with no pain, cramps, or exhaustion, it wouldn't have been nearly the same.

I had to hurt and want to give up, yet still not give in. I had to gasp and barely breathe. I had to cramp. I had to question myself and my abilities. I had to climb. That peak was my cause beyond all comfort, and I was going to take it. No matter what. Every ounce of physical and mental energy I had at the time was the price to summit.

It was time to climb again.

It was time to get up and get on with it.

It was time to take the reins of my own leadership. It was time to put cowering and self-pity and victim mentality behind.

---

*Circumstances don't make a man, they reveal him.*

---

I began taking my freedom back—regardless of my circumstances. You see, liberty can be taken, but freedom can only be given away. It was time to take the freedom and power back. In prison, I might have been known as 267823, but that was *not* who I was. I was so much more than that.

## CHAPTER 2

# LEADERS ARE NOT BORN, THEY ARE BUILT

*"Leadership is confusing as hell."*
**—Tom Peters**

I grew up as a scrawny, insecure, introverted kid with crooked buck teeth and Coke-bottle glasses. And if that wasn't bad enough, I was also the son of a very captivating, dynamic, and domineering Protestant minister. A natural introvert, I found myself forced into my own internal cave of inadequacy as a child. I was as opposite to stereotypical leader material as you can imagine.

As a result, I always strove to prove myself to myself, to my dad, and to the world. When I was just six years old, I got my first job. I stood on the corner of the local grocery store all day Saturday and Sunday after church selling *Grit* newspaper.

"America's Greatest Family Newspaper" was printed proudly on the paper's masthead. The irony of the title *Grit* speaks volumes. Little did I know how much grit I would need to develop and possess throughout the balance of my life. My family was far from great or perfect. I guess no family really is. After years of working with clients from all over the world, I've realized that most people share this sentiment.

We lost my father to a hard-fought battle with Alzheimer's in 2016. Though I never would have believed it as a child, my dad became central to both my personal development as a leader and the evolution of my leadership style.

My dad was both charismatic and overbearing. He never knew how to make his family feel loved. Many men don't. At least he didn't make me feel loved. I never had any training in compassion growing up because my dad didn't really have any. For his parishioners, maybe, but certainly not for me. This was not his fault. His dad, my grandfather, didn't have any either.

The sins of the fathers are visited on the sons.

As painful as this was, I'm grateful for the gifts it brought me: self-reliance, resilience, and independence, just to name a few. Remember, pain is the mother of all growth. My first introduction to deep emotional pain came early in life.

I greatly feared my dad as a child, but as an adult I came to understand and respect him. He was, and always will be, one of my greatest mentors.

## Great Mentors Create Great Leaders

Every great leader has had a mentor. Steve Jobs had Andy Grove, Mark Zuckerberg had Steve Jobs, Bill Gates had Warren Buffett, John Coltrane had Charlie Parker and Dennis Sandole, Alexander the Great had Aristotle, Michael Jordan had Dean Smith, and Leonardo da Vinci had Andrea del Verrochio. The list is endless.

*Leaders are built, not born.*

My dad was on the admiral's staff in the Navy. He was a Golden Gloves boxer and an outstanding basketball player. I heard his stories over and over again, more times than I could count. Every time I heard them, it drove the pain of my own inadequacy deeper. I was the polar opposite. Dad was also verbose and social; he loved to talk about himself. He had a countless number of great achievements. I had no big victories. None.

My father never thought I was good enough, but he was a hero in my young eyes. Years later, I grew to have deep compassion for my dad, for I now know that *he* didn't feel good enough. For *him* it was never enough.

The Church of God is similar to the Southern Baptist Church. They're both on the extreme fundamental side of the Christian faith. My dad was a very successful pastor in the Church of God, and he was an extremely theatrical preacher. Out from behind the podium he bounded, kicking his leg up into the air and slamming his Bible on the podium.

He didn't preach as much as he roared.

He was also openly emotive and often cried onstage when he was particularly inspired. That made a huge impact on me as a little boy. Contrary to what most men learn, I learned it was okay to show and express emotion. I'm grateful for that.

When I was a young kid, a lot of things he would say to me lacked compassion, but I now know it wasn't intentional. It's just who he was. He was doing the best he could with the resources he'd been handed. It was who his dad was as well. As an adult, I came to understand that my grandad never treated my dad very well.

Although dad was never physically abusive, it was often a different story verbally and emotionally. I really didn't understand his behavior as a child. What I now realize is that people who don't feel good about themselves must lower others to raise themselves. They feebly attempt to make themselves feel better by making others feel worse.

---

*Hurt people hurt other people.*

---

In my mind, my dad was a hero and I was a zero. I was always in his shadow. Yet, no matter how much my dad accomplished, he still didn't feel good about himself. And, for his field and profession, he accomplished immense results. He was pretty much the go-to guy in the Church of God. But again, it wasn't enough.

That's what my dad did, because that's what my grandfather did. It's just what he knew. That's how my dad was programmed and conditioned, and therefore so was I.

## Your Leadership Style Is a Byproduct of Where You Have Been

Multiple types of leadership styles are available to choose from. Some work depending on the situation and environment, and some don't work at all.

My dad's brand of leadership was "command and control." In other words, he used positional power, leadership based in fear, which can only work in the near-term. It's human nature. Eventually, we no longer accept being threatened or frightened. At some point, another person can no longer exert the power of their position over us.

"Do as I say because I'm the boss." That's the core of command and control leadership. It's how I was raised. The answer to why was, "Because I said so." It's what I knew; it was the only card in my early leadership deck.

Ultimately, that type of leadership doesn't work for anyone, especially the younger generations. Our future is a generation of young adults who push back against authority and strive for autonomy when it comes to work and career. That's actually a great thing when understood and utilized—it just means the older generations need to rethink their leadership approach.

---

*One of the greatest leadership skills we all*
*must develop is the ability to reinvent ourselves.*

---

True leadership is much more than "Do what I say because I said to do it." Perhaps that's a lesson we can learn from the generations following us. They seem to already understand that this approach doesn't work.

Every generation produced, or is producing, different types of leaders. It must be this way. By and large, you're the byproduct of other people's habitual ways of thinking: your parents, your school system, your church, your government, your peer group, and society at large.

My parents were a product of the Silent Generation. Their generation ran up more debt in their time in leadership because they never had to confront difficulty. They were like dolphins. Dolphins are really smart, yet they have no natural enemies or predators to outwit; thus, they never sharpen their natural abilities. After all, the battle to survive and thrive is what makes us bigger, better, and stronger.

---

*Confronting challenges builds more resilience, resourcefulness, creativity, intelligence, and grit.*

---

The Silent Generation were severely weakened by their upbringing and lifestyle. Why wouldn't they be? They grew up in the shadow of WWII heroes and Great Depression survivors, yet they had no idea what it meant to build resilience and resourcefulness for themselves. They never had to. They watched their parents struggle and rebuild the entire United States. Talk about learning to persevere through difficulties and tough times. The World War II generation took care of business. They didn't have any other choice.

Generation X and the Millennials are the first generations in history predicted to make less money than their parents. Is it any wonder they're pissed off and angry? Is it any mystery that Generation X helped spawn the angry grunge music scene? They're a generation founded in anger. Millennials have the *potential* to be the greatest leaders we've ever had—world leaders versus "just my country" leaders. But they'll have to *drastically* transform their mindset to accomplish this. Facing adversity and playing the long-game is not a favorite for Millennials. But that's what it takes.

Most recent research proves that the majority of Millennials spend 50 percent of their day surfing the internet and living in devastating distraction, waiting for their "big break" when they'll become the next Justin Bieber or Kardashian just by flipping up a video on YouTube. Nowhere is this more rampant than with Millennials.

But it's not just Millennials—it's Gen X and Boomers too! We live in a society of fast fame, get-rich-quick gimmicks, of secret sauce and simple success. Everyone wants to be redeemed, but they're unwilling to pay the price of redemption.

These may not sound like the best leadership traits, which they aren't, but they do have the potential to shift us all into strong and effective *world* leaders. In this age of the entrepreneur, none of us want to be told what to do or what not to do. We want to be the leaders. Most have entrepreneurial aspirations because they don't want to go to work and report to someone else. They want to report to themselves or have people reporting to them, in their own business.

Entrepreneurs change the world, and we're grooming a generation of potentially great entrepreneurial world leaders. The question is, what is being done to encourage this? What is being done to help every individual realize their gifts and potential?

## Current Leaders and Systems Are Failing

We're all products of *both* nature and nurture. We're all born with certain gifts, but at the same time we're all conditioned by our environment. Our God-given gifts are what make us leaders—all special and unique leaders—so much more than the roles we have been conditioned to play.

Think of our education system today. What happens when a kid is struggling in math? What do we tell them? Work harder at math. Study more math. Is that really the best approach?

What we need to be telling them is to forget about math and instead put their energy and time into perfecting the subjects they *are* good at. If you put all your energy and effort from trying to improve your B game into mastering your A game, you could lead the field in the area where you have gifts. This is where the leadership of the future must be built. This is the new approach that begs to be applied.

---

*Those who follow the crowd most often get absolutely lost in it.*

---

It's time we tap into our gifts and move beyond the comfort zone of "nurture." We have to step out of what we know and step into a world that's often unknown, uncomfortable, and scary. We all have the gifts to transform how we've been conditioned. We all have potential to be disruptive and live more creatively than what we've been given as the norm.

That's exactly what I've had to do time and time again.

## A Force of Nature Called Justin

When I was in prison, one of the rules was that you didn't mess with Justin. He had a dark, disturbing sort of Charles Manson look in his eyes. He had a completely shaved head with a large red swastika tattooed across the entirety of his skull. Chilling. I swung wide of him whenever possible. One afternoon as I was reading on my bunk, I looked up, sensing a presence, and he was standing in my doorway. Another cultural norm in prison was you never stepped into another man's "house" without asking permission. He asked if he could come in and talk with me.

"Sure," I said reluctantly. What else could I say?

He sauntered in with a gangster-like forward slump that signaled, "You don't want to mess with me." He scanned the environment, checking for potential danger, surprise, or ambush; his lifestyle had taught him to be ever on guard. Unlike the dolphin, he *had* known predators and plenty of them. He was like an animal sniffing and scanning for danger. I was on the bottom bunk. He eyed the concrete stool a few feet away, waiting for an invitation to sit. This too was protocol, and even the toughest of men followed it.

"Have a seat," I said.

He sat down, and I swung around so I was sitting up, facing him. The guy was a killer, a frightening, angry man, and I wondered why he had sought me out.

"I don't really know why I'm here," he began awkwardly. "But, you know, I'm getting out soon."

"Yeah, I heard that," I said.

"And I haven't been sleeping at all. I'm having these weird nightmares and just . . . I don't know why. I'm excited to be getting out. But . . ."

It took me about two heartbeats to figure out that he was scared. He was the big dog in prison. He got anything he wanted within these walls. But outside, he had nothing.

"I just don't know who else in here to talk to about this," he confessed with surprising vulnerability and sincerity.

"Justin, let me tell you something," I said. "I was scared shitless when I came here. I didn't know what was going to happen to me. I thought I might get raped, stabbed, or beaten up. I didn't know if I could make it. And now here I am. How do you think I'm doing?"

"I think you're doing alright," he said.

"Thank you," I said. "I think I've adapted. I'm doing okay. I don't know if I have it all figured out, but I'm navigating this environment."

I paused.

"Let me ask you, Justin, given the way you grew up compared to the way I grew up, what do you think the chances are that you and I would be sitting right here, right now in this cell, having this conversation?"

I couldn't imagine a more opposite nurture experience than mine and Justin's.

"Slim to none," he said. He was brutal but incredibly smart.

"Right. Yet here we are."

I paused again and did something I had rarely done since arriving at Eagle Point. I stared straight at Justin as if we were equals, straight into his eyes.

"You know what I was most scared of when I got here, Justin?"

"What?"

"You."

He nodded and smirked.

"Not literally you because, obviously, I didn't know you then. But everything you represent was so foreign to me, and frightening, and now here I am. I've come into your world, and I'm doing okay."

"Yeah, you're doing okay."

"And now you're going out into my world. And you know what you're scared of?"

"What?"

"Me."

He let out a small grunt. This was a guy who was "afraid of no man."

I let that sit for a second.

"Not literally me, but everything I represent. But you know what? I came in here and figured out your world, and now, if you want, you can figure out mine. Here's the reality. I know if I piss you off, you can take me out right here, right now. I know that for a fact and so do you. No question. But you know what else I know? A gorilla could do that. And you're more than that, Justin. You're a sharp, intelligent guy. But if you keep acting like a gorilla, you won't succeed in my world. If you adopt a new strategy, if you use your intelligence to figure out my world, you'll do okay. If I can figure out your world, Justin, you can figure out mine. You can do it. You've got this."

He sat for a few moments, absorbing the conversation, shaking his head as if trying to shake off an old skin. Then he stood up.

"Well, I gotta go get some lunch," he responded abruptly.

And he walked out.

What I realized in that moment was that Justin and I were the same guy. At the highest level of awareness, we all have much the same nature. We're scared of the same things—the unknown, life's uncertainties. Justin and I had just chosen different ways to deal with our common issues.

We've given away our ability to truly lead in most cases and have become nothing but pawns of the system in which we're imprisoned. In a very real sense, we lead the lives that Thoreau spoke of so clearly, "lives of quiet desperation"— regardless of how loud we bark and how big we blow.

It was a major eye-opener for me, one of social scientist Dr. Morris Massey's "Significant Emotional Events" of the grandest magnitude.

Realizing the human condition was the same for everyone was a profound moment for me, maybe one of my most profound moments ever. Something inside of me shifted.

It shifted hard.

From that moment on, I looked at these guys so differently. In fact, at all of humanity differently. I suddenly realized we are all on the same ship, navigating the same waters. Currently, I was in the boiler room on the ship of humanity.

In the boiler room we cuss, we fight. It's dirty and dark. We jostle for position and power through sheer physical force. We tattoo ourselves with our gang affiliates and our "badges of honor." And we do *all* of this in a feeble attempt to minimize the pain and suffering we find inside ourselves.

In the penthouse of the very same ship, we're desperately trying to escape the exact same fears and issues. We "tattoo" ourselves with expensive jewelry and watches, we cheat with our business partner's wife, we embezzle money to buy the latest Prada or Bentley. Instead of physical power, we use the power of intelligence to outwit and outsmart and possibly manipulate others. Yet the nagging little splinter in the back of our mind does not quit nagging and festering, and the exact same suffering continues.

The pain is the same. The only difference is that we're all coping with different tools and equipment. We're all the products of our own unique conditioning and norms. The nurture of our social programming has us by the throat and provides no quarter. Nearly all of us are afraid to step beyond The Resistance inside ourselves to explore what we don't know.

We're all faced with reinvention in today's world. Jobs are going away and being replaced by AIs and robots. Many are waking up in their fifties and finding themselves without a job and little to no savings. It's hard enough to reinvent yourself in your thirties. It feels nearly impossible for those in their fifties.

Just as I had to reinvent myself and assimilate into a new culture to survive in prison, and just as Justin had to reinvent himself to function in the world outside of barbed wire and guards, so we all must reinvent ourselves daily to survive and thrive in a rapidly changing world. This is fundamental to leading our lives and fulfilling our potential.

We can argue and hang on to "the way it used to be" as much as we like, but unless we adapt, we won't survive. It must start with our viewpoint and then be followed by behavior.

---

*Our greatest opportunities reside just beyond our greatest fears.*

---

Until we find the courage to take that step, we continue in quiet desperation. Selling ourselves short and selling ourselves out.

## It's Your Life, so Start Leading It

If we all do the best we can with the resources we have, then falling short is a lack of abilities and resources more than a lack of character. This is a very important lesson for leadership on all levels to learn and remember.

My dad's goal for me was to join the ministry, to follow in his footsteps as a preacher. He had it all lined up for me. He had my whole life figured out.

Then I woke up one day and thought, *I don't want to be a preacher.*

I was born with the drive to accomplish something. From the time I got that very first job at six years old, I wanted to do something meaningful, to contribute something significant. I was always fulfilled by work and my contribution. I always knew I was put here to do something unique, even though I didn't know exactly what that unique something was.

I used to think I was the only one who felt that inner drive to greatness. I now know that we all feel, at some level, this deep sense of purpose and destiny, though maybe some feel it more than others.

Unfortunately, my experience has proven that while most feel this drive, very few ever embark on the journey to fulfill it. The price to be paid is just too high. But that drive is still with me to this day. For whatever reason, I've always had an attraction to hard work.

## Finding My Own True Grit

As soon as I got my driver's license, I used the money I had socked away to buy a motorcycle. Then I signed up for *two* morning paper routes. That was the beginning of my practice of getting up at four o'clock—a practice which continues to this day. To say the paper routes were brutal is an understatement. Winters in Oklahoma are full of snow and lots of it.

My younger brother, Jon, and I were four years apart and always close. He was probably my best friend growing up, more the result of proximity and my introversion than shared values or common interests. Our temperaments are quite different, yet he was my best friend. We're still extremely close to this day. I think he's always understood me more than most, though we're so different.

Now he works with his hands remodeling homes. I work with my mind and heart remodeling lives. Yet we share the same DNA and were raised in the same environment by the same parents. We shared the same nurture, but our natures are drastically different. The gifts we were given are drastically different, almost diametrically opposed.

Keeping up with two early morning paper routes would be challenging for any sixteen-year-old, but it was especially so for me. For me, school never came easily, which meant staying up studying late into the night.

That wasn't the only part of school that was tough for me. I always felt odd, like I didn't fit in, and I struggled to connect with any of the other kids because I never felt as though we shared the same values.

I was never very athletic, but I still tried out for sports because it was the thing to do. Of course, this was just an exercise in futility because I never made the teams. Talk about pouring fuel on the fire of already low self-esteem.

What I lacked in physical coordination and athleticism I made up for in a passion for research and learning. I was constantly reading. I think I truly believed that if I could just find the answers to life and uncover how the universe really worked, somehow my life would be different, happier; I could be more confident and fulfilled. Maybe then I would find my place in the world instead of circling on the fringe like an outsider. So, while everyone else was out playing baseball or going to dances and movies, I was perfectly happy being alone in my bedroom. Reading.

After high school and into my early twenties, I got into competitive bodybuilding. I saw it as my ticket to significance, a way out of the cave of my own inadequacies. Of course, my dad thought it was the most ridiculous thing ever. He didn't mince words when he told me that either.

I remember walking into Mike Moguin's gym in Tulsa, Oklahoma. Mike Moguin was a bodybuilder, probably in his late thirties or early forties at the time. I went up to the counter and asked about membership. He asked me a few questions, and I told him I wanted to get into bodybuilding. He looked me over and said, "You'll never be a bodybuilder."

He said I would never make it because I didn't have the right build or genetics. While he was right, his delivery was brutal. My feelings of insecurity and inadequacy erupted. It was coming from all sides now, and I saw no escape.

It hurt, but as usual during that time, I didn't have anything to say in response. I did, however, say to myself, *You just watch. I'm going to show you.* And, for whatever reason, Mike Moguin's words only strengthened my resolve.

Sure, it would have been easy to crawl back into my cave and fade away, but I didn't. I buckled down and worked hard—much harder, much longer than the guys with good genetics were working. I didn't know it at the time, but this was the birth of a major theme in my life story.

---

*You have to be willing to go up against all odds stacked against you.*

---

I remember a guy posting on Facebook in 2013, after one of my first social media posts after my release, "Good to hear from you, James; you're the comeback king." While this may seem exciting, strong, or sexy at some level, what it meant to me was that to "comeback" I had to have fallen and fallen hard.

## True Leaders Go All-In

---

*"Don't start a business unless it's an obsession.*
*If you have an exit strategy, it's not an obsession."*
**—Mark Cuban**

---

I worked out obsessively, bound and determined to prove Mike Moguin's predictions wrong. I worked out twice a day—two hours in the morning and two hours again each night, six days a week.

It became my sole reason for being.

I pushed more weights around the gym than a wrecking crew. I went from 6-foot-1, 150 pounds soaking wet, to a 220-pound strapping, well-built young man—on the outside. On the inside, I still felt like the same introverted, insecure guy.

Several years later, I won the light heavyweight Mr. Oklahoma contest. I really don't have the structure to be a great bodybuilder; Moguin was right. But I overcame that setback with drive, discipline, and commitment.

*When all odds seem stacked against you, get excited.*
*That means the victory will be that much sweeter.*

Looking back, it all seems pretty shallow. However, that doesn't change the tremendous impact that experience had on my life. I was able to take the habits of discipline and overcoming adversity into my entrepreneurial adventure.

This was when I first came to truly realize that pain is the mother of all growth. If you can learn to transmute the pain into purpose, suffering into significance, and learn to love the burn, you know the soreness is telling you that you're doing something meaningful. What a great metaphor for life.

After I won the light heavyweight Mr. Oklahoma, I continued competing. One day I was standing onstage and looked down at myself. I was oiled up, ripped to shreds, and devoid of any body fat. I had dieted and trained hard.

I looked at the guy on my left and the guy on my right and then surveyed the big audience and the judges. It dawned on me: *What the hell am I doing? I'm standing here half naked in front of hundreds of people, and some of these other guys can't even spell their own name. I'm not judging them—I know them! And the judges couldn't care less whether I can even construct an intelligible sentence. I've got way more going for me than this. What the hell am I doing?*

I wanted to run off the stage. I didn't, but it would be my last appearance on a bodybuilding stage. It finally hit me that I had been putting all my time and energy into something transitory. I gave everything I had for something that could be gone in a second.

This was the first step in my realization that I was meant for more, that my gifts were something much deeper and more profound than anything I could have accomplished in the gym or up there on that particular stage.

That was the first step. The second was to come in the form of disaster, and it changed my perspective on life in an instant.

## It's Not Supposed to Be Easy

---

*It's not supposed to be easy. It's supposed to be meaningful.*

---

For the first two years of college, I worked three part time jobs and was taking sixteen hours of classes. I had to work because I was paying my own rent, bills, car payment, and tuition.

I was eighteen when I moved out of my parents' house. That was a real coming-of-age moment for me. I had never gone against my dad's wishes before. I never went back home either, until I was forced to by a life tsunami at age fifty-one. But that's getting ahead of the story.

From the moment I moved out, I was on a mission to make my mark. Multiple jobs later—holding two to three at a time—quitting college after my second year, I finally landed a job at AT&T and my career was on a climb. I held various sales jobs for them, ran numerous phone center stores, got transferred to Kansas City from Tulsa, ran their national telemarketing office, and eventually became a National Sales Trainer. I bought a nice new home in Kansas City and all my hard work seemed to be paying off.

All along I was still working out obsessively in the gym as well. Up to four hours per day.

In the late 1980s, I was in a horrible motorcycle accident and landed in intensive care for six weeks: breakdown, turnaround, lose it all, keep pushing forward, comeback king. It's the story of my life.

I was on my brand-new Kawasaki Ninja late one night heading from downtown Kansas City. Coming around a hard right-hand curve, I was hit head-on by a car and shattered my left forearm. Later I was told that the sound of the collision awakened people in their beds over a block away.

I woke up in intensive care. The collision blew out my knees and several discs in my lower and upper back. Over the course of those six weeks in ICU, I had eight surgeries on my left arm and almost lost my left hand twice. They told me I would never lift weights again as I quickly went from 220 pounds of pure muscle to 170 pounds of insecure, destroyed, and deflated human being.

This was a true moment of clarity. I suddenly knew that it was time to take a step back, evaluate my life, and really, really think about what I was giving my time and energy to. What was I trading my life for?

## What Are You Trading Your Life For?

You see, we all trade our life for something. To be the true leader of your life, you must ensure you're trading your life for something worth trading it for.

It's ironic that my life has been a continuous series of crash-and-burns followed by turnaround and coming back stronger. My MO is turnaround, comeback, and rebuild higher than ever before.

It's a tough truth to swallow that every breakthrough in your life is preceded by a breakdown. Destruction is the first step before any construction begins.

*When you hit rock bottom, you've finally found a firm foundation from which to build.*

You see, I'm no different from you. We all deal with the same challenges, doubts, and dilemmas. The only difference is by degree. Every person's hardest thing is *their* hardest thing. It's all relative.

After my recovery, I continued to work out. I obviously was unable to do it with the same intensity as I had when I was competing, but I was still at the gym every day. In fact, I still work out every day. The discipline, energy, and vitality it brings me is invaluable. The neuro-cocktails a hard workout releases, like dopamine, serotonin, norepinephrine, and others, enhance creativity, engagement, focus, and the ability not to "lose it" through challenges as you find creative solutions.

As an entrepreneur, I see working out as part of my job. I encourage this mindset with my executive coaching clients as well. It takes tremendous discipline, energy, and vitality to build a business, build a life, and then help others build theirs. You're not going to be able to accomplish it all with low physical energy; you need strength and power for the long haul.

---

*It always takes twice as long as you predict and normally costs twice as much.*

---

Getting fired from a construction job after leaving college ended up being the best thing that ever happened to me. That's when I landed my job at AT&T. I couldn't articulate it back then, but by now I've grown to understand that all pain, once unwrapped, contains a gift.

---

*Always expect the best, and realize the best is often what you initially perceive as the worst.*

---

That constant reminder helped me through the experience in the Arizona courtroom and with prison as well. Don't get me wrong. It all was incredibly dark and hard, and I'd never want to do any of it again. But I'm grateful for the lessons learned, which I believe couldn't have been learned any other way.

At the construction job, I had been delivering sheet rock to Southwestern Bell in Tulsa, a then subsidiary of AT&T, so I got to know a couple of people in the office as I went there every day. After getting fired, I decided to get cleaned up, go back to Southwestern Bell, and apply for a job. To my surprise and delight,

I got hired to work in the telemarketing department, and I immediately excelled, becoming one of the top salespeople.

## Finding My Purpose and My Flow

On the day of my second anniversary with Southwestern Bell, I got promoted to train new telemarketers. The minute I stood in front of that room to give my first training presentation, I knew I had found my home. It felt magical. I took stories and illustrations from my own life experiences and wove them into the training and made it exciting. I loved it.

I looked around the room and realized I was moving people. They were engaged. I thought, *Damn, this feels awesome.* Everything made sense in that moment. My spirit was expressing a desire to be onstage—not to entertain but to educate.

Mihaly Csikszentmihalyi, professor of psychology and management at Claremont Graduate University, has conducted extensive research on a state he calls "flow." William James called it a mystical state. Abraham Maslow called it a peak state. Csikszentmihalyi modernized it into the flow state.

Flow is an extremely productive state of living, performing, and achieving. In fact, Csikszentmihalyi calls it, "The psychology of optimal experience."

The flow state is the best way for me to describe my experience in front of that room. You know you're kicking ass, but you're not quite sure you're the one doing the kicking. It's humbling, if you're wise. If you get arrogant and start to think it's you, you cut off the flow because it's *not* you, not really, not the ego personality "you" anyway. It's something much greater and grander.

Flow comes from a place of tapping into something bigger. That's how it felt for me the first time. That first day at Southwestern Bell, I sure got a taste of it. And it's addictive.

*Oh my God, I found my home!*

I didn't always get back into flow, and I still don't. But when I do, it's a high.

I moved from sales trainer to sales manager. It was a promotion. It was more money, but the new position wasn't what I loved doing. Even though I was good at it, I missed my position in training and development.

---

*Life and leadership are not about money. They're about meaning.*

---

It's about meaning. It's about doing what you love. Every one of us has a unique genius and purpose in life. I trust you've figured out that you're at the top of your game and are most fulfilled when you're using your unique gifts and doing what you're here to do, especially when you've developed the skills to do it well.

We live in a world that's all about fast fame and simple success, without concern for the skills to back it up. We've become conditioned to think that we love something because it's highly valued by society's standards.

We have to remember to think for ourselves, and this is much easier in theory than it is in practice.

## Leadership or Positional Power?

In this first leadership role, my biggest mistake was letting my team's success breed cockiness. My overly confident attitude only made things worse with my peers, who were all twice my age. I've learned that any time you get cocky, you're losing sight of the gifts you've been given and the power that's working *through* you versus *from* you. Big difference. You lose your flow.

The old adage "Pride comes before a fall" isn't just an adage. It's the truth.

---

*When you start to think you're the bomb,*
*life teaches you what it's like to get bombed.*

---

I went into my leadership roles at AT&T with the leadership style I'd been nurtured with from childhood. All I knew was the "do as I say" leadership model. That was my norm. I didn't know any other way. In fact, that's how I went into my first marriage as well. That type of leadership doesn't work in business or in life. Positional power is not true leadership.

But my thinking was starting to shift. I was learning that engagement and ownership brought vastly more, not just *from* people but from *within* people. You can hire hands. But no amount of money can hire heart.

It took a tremendous amount of self-awareness and self-exploration for me to discover this fundamental leadership principle. If you have not yet learned that positional power is not leadership, please listen to the voice of experience. Learn from my mistakes.

I asked myself, *How can I develop my leadership and find new role models who can help me get to where I want to be, need to be, and know I can be?*

## The Value of a Leadership Mentor

Though I didn't know it at the time, my dad was my first real mentor. At AT&T, I found my second influential mentor. Ron Crenshaw was my boss, but he was also my first *business* mentor and coach. He was the role model I was looking for as I adjusted my leadership style.

Ron had a tremendous impact on my leadership skills. He was collaborative, conversational, and empowering, with a quiet strength about him. His style made you feel that he cared for you, yet you also knew you had to pull your weight. He had a way of making you *want to* versus feel like you *had to*.

That's where I wanted to be. That's where I needed to be, and Ron helped me make that shift.

---

*Leaders are built by the role models and mentors they seek out. They are open to being guided and corrected because feedback is the breakfast of champions.*

---

If you're going to climb Mount Everest, you had better have a great guide, one who has done it multiple times before. You don't want someone who's read books on it or studied it in college. You need the person who has actually *done* it!

Likewise, if you're on the journey to become a leader, you absolutely need a mentor and guide who is further down the particular path you're wanting to walk.

All of us have the same human traits available to us. We all develop these traits differently, but they're all there in our arsenal of tools to use as we develop as individuals. Each trait has intrinsic value. However, any trait—good or bad—developed to an extreme becomes a vice, and it's a fine line between virtue and vice.

That's why it's so important to find harmony. We can't focus on developing just one trait, no matter how redeeming that trait may be. If you only have one card to play, you don't have much of a hand, now do you?

This is where a good mentor and coach is invaluable. It's next to impossible to get enough distance from your own nonsense to see yourself clearly. You need objective and caring input from someone who cares enough not to make you *feel* better, but to make you *be* better!

---

*The best feedback is not what you want to hear but what you need to hear.*

---

The way you lead your own life and the way you work through your own issues is the way you will show up for others, especially in leadership. How you do anything is how you do everything. In both life and leadership, you only play with the deck you have. If your deck is limited, you're destined to lose. Get a better deck.

I had nowhere near the experience or tenure of my peers. Most had years on me in terms of experience and age. I was missing a lot of cards from my deck, but I didn't realize that back then.

At that time, I was the poster child for positional power. I was insecure, so I had to prove myself constantly. With all my effort, I still knew I didn't have a lot of real power. Deep inside, I felt pretty much like an empty title.

It seems so obvious now, like it was such a simple lesson, but I promise you, it wasn't. I couldn't learn without a lot of falling down and getting back up, without many mistakes and corrections, without trial and error. Old habits of thoughts, feelings, and actions die hard. It takes time.

One day it just hit me: *If I could lead through inspiration and ownership rather than fear, and bring something of value to the table, then maybe, just maybe, I could get people to perform to the best of their ability.* No matter if they had positional ownership or a title or not, if I could make them *feel* like they did, then maybe that would become *their* norm.

## Returning to Flow

In my final position at AT&T, I was transferred to the AT&T School of Business in Atlanta. That was a brilliant move. At this point, I was in charge of all management training and business consulting for the nation, working with C-Suite executives and their teams. It didn't take long before I was the top producer in the AT&T School of Business.

In 1991, AT&T was going through major restructuring and downsizing, and they came out with a program that would allow employees to take a five-year leave of absence with a return position guaranteed. During the five-year leave, the company would pay for insurance and for us to finish our education. This was a golden opportunity, and I was primed to seize it.

I was just five hours short of a bachelor's degree in applied behavioral sciences. When I first began college, I studied business management for the first two years. Dad told me that was the route to go, and as an obedient son, I followed. I always felt a little insecure that I had not finished my degree, particularly working in a corporate management environment where I was one of the few who hadn't.

When I went back to night school, I finally studied what I loved and was good at: applied behavioral sciences. Now, finally, I was just one elective short of my bachelor's degree.

For me, leadership, influence, coaching, consulting, and oral presentations all fell under the umbrella of human behavior. What is it that moves people emotionally, mentally, and physically to take action? What brings influence?

Because of my analytical mind, answering these questions has always been a game for me, and I thoroughly enjoy it.

When flow is working through me, I feel it. And flow can occur for me whether it's on the phone or in person. I'm a natural at sales, coaching, consulting, and oral presentations—even though I got a *C* in college speech class. Go figure. My insecurities got the best of me, and I was petrified.

My intention was to work on a master's degree in behavioral sciences, and in my mind this was a brilliant opportunity. I thought, *This leave of absence they're offering is a good opportunity, because I want to start my own business anyway. This is the way for me to achieve multiple objectives.*

I signed up to take the leave program, and the clock started ticking. First I would go back to finish my degree on AT&T's dime.

Not so fast.

Almost immediately, I got a large consulting contract with a subsidiary of AT&T in Little Rock, Arkansas. I was thrilled because I thought to myself, *Okay, I'm leaving. I've got insurance paid, I've got a guaranteed safety net, I can come back in five years, and I've got a client. So I'm set.* But I had not read the fine print.

The leave of absence agreement specified that you could not work with AT&T or any of its subsidiaries while you were on leave. Now I faced a conundrum. I wondered, *Do I take the contract and cancel the leave, or do I take the safety net and let the contract go?*

## Leaders Follow Intuition and Instinct

I wrestled with the decision because I was frightened of making the wrong choice. I finally had to ask myself, *What do I really want to do?* My gut told me, *I want to have my own business.* I didn't like people placing their limitations on me and telling me what to do. I certainly didn't want them telling me what I couldn't do or spend to perform at world-class levels for my clients. I was tired of all the politics, rules, regulations, and red tape.

Then I asked myself the question, *Okay, I want to have my own business, so do I really want to come back to AT&T in five years?* The answer was no. *What I really want to do is succeed and succeed big.* The next question was, *Why am I being so fearful? Have faith in yourself. Just do it!*

Leaders must make decisions with the information they have. Decisions are risky and consequences follow. But the greatest risk in today's world is taking no risk at all.

---

*Taking risk is not about taking a big chance,*
*3it's about giving yourself a big chance.*

---

That's exactly what I did. I went into my boss's office the next day and told her I wasn't taking the leave. I was going to quit instead. I handed her my resignation. Her jaw dropped. She asked, "Are you sure?"

I said, "Yes, I'm absolutely sure. I'm just going to go for it."

To say I was nervous would be an understatement. I was wrestling with myself, rehearsing my perceived limitations and doubts over and over in my mind. But I knew it was now or never.

I took the leap. I left AT&T and went out on my own. When I first left, I did business consulting work, and it was a great year. I tripled my salary from AT&T, which was more than I ever imagined I would make.

I went home for Christmas at the end of that first year. I was on top of the world because nobody in my family had ever made that much money in one year. I remember sitting in my parents' living room, and it suddenly hit me that come January first, I was starting at zero again. My one-year contract had ended, and I didn't have another one in the works. I was unemployed. I had to start over—a concept all entrepreneurs experience at least once in their journey.

I fell apart in my parents' living room. I was petrified. Ironically, doing so incredibly well that first year actually made it *more* frightening. I asked myself, *How will I ever repeat that? How can I ever do it again? What if I don't do anything?* I was overcome with self-doubt. It was terrifying.

However, the worry was unwarranted. The next year my income increased by a little over 25 percent, and I just kept climbing. I was off and running. For me, it was never about the money, it was about the work; it was about the sense of accomplishment; it was about contributing and doing something that felt meaningful.

Even later, when I was making millions of dollars per year, the money was never what drove me. It was more about the craft and the product and service. Most important, it was about the feeling of fulfillment as I helped people in their lives and businesses and watched their results shift. I would think, *Look at this brilliant video program we put together, how it moves people and how the audience is impacted.*

Anyone who knows me knows that I love to make money *only* to use it as a tool to do bigger and more creative things. I believe we're all hardwired to be creative in our own way. True leadership is more art than science. We're all artists at heart. For art resides in the heart.

## True Leadership Requires Quick Decisions

I decided to make the big move from Atlanta to La Jolla, California. At the time, more professional speakers and trainers were in one square mile of La Jolla than anywhere else in the world. I thought, *That's where I need to be.*

I went to La Jolla on a business trip. Driving down La Jolla Scenic Drive for the first time, I came around a corner and saw the ocean and La Jolla spread out in front of me. I said to myself, *I can catch a plane from here as well as I can catch one from anywhere else, so I'm going to move here.* I found a real estate agent and made an offer on a home the next day—even though I still had to sell my house in Atlanta.

---

*Once they have the information that's available, true leaders make quick decisions.*

---

True leaders make quick decisions. We don't need more data, we need more intuition. Leaders realize that you must make decisions with the information you have. If those decisions must be tweaked, changed, or improved upon later, so be it. But it's always better to do *something*, even if hindsight says it was "wrong."

Often you must make a decision with the information you have and then hope there's a forgiving God.

I moved in eight weeks. I was off to find my great adventure. I got to La Jolla and said, *Here I am, world. Swoop me up.* Except it didn't exactly happen as quickly as I'd expected.

I quadrupled my overhead by moving to La Jolla. I thought I had it covered because I already had two big consulting contracts in the bag when I got there—more than enough to carry me through the entire next year, I reasoned.

## My Next Business Mentors

Upon arrival, I got on the phone and called everybody who was a celebrity speaker at the time: Tony Alessandra, Brian Tracy, Jim Cathcart, Ken Blanchard, Tony Robbins, and many others. The only one who took my call was Tony Alessandra. This would prove to be a monumental point in my journey.

Tony had no idea who I was. I said, "Hey, I've just moved here from Atlanta, and I want to come meet you and talk with you." He was so far beyond anything I could conceive at the time that it felt like I was talking to royalty.

At his office in downtown La Jolla, I remember sitting across the table as we made our introductions, and he said, "What can I do for you?"

I said, "Nothing really. I just want to know you."

He flinched in surprise. But I meant it.

I said, "Tell me what you're doing and what's going on in your business."

As always, I asked a lot of questions. He showed me a new corporate training program he'd just created. I told him I had several corporate clients and could probably sell his program to some of them.

It took him completely off-guard. He later told me, "Everyone who has ever come to my office has wanted something *from* me. You were the first person who offered to *help me*!"

Leaders always work to provide ten times more value than what they ask for in return. They don't ask, "What can I get?" Rather, "What can I give?" Remember, all true leaders are committed to a purpose far beyond themselves and their own personal needs. This is the price of true leadership.

Now, when I talk to people about approaching potential mentors, I suggest they bring value to the mentor first. For me, it was not strategically thought out at the time. I wish I could say it was, but it just wasn't. I was just genuinely excited to be in Tony's office and to meet him.

Tony and I quickly became fast friends, and we still are to this day. He was one of the very few people—I can count them on one hand—who stood with me during the storm of 2009. When you find these people, hang on to them and cherish them. They're rare indeed.

Tony was so far ahead of me in his speaking business that he became an incredible mentor for me in those early years. This was an area of business that was brand new to me. Years later, I asked him why he helped me so much. He said, "I really loved your energy, and I liked the fact that you were willing to help sell some of my programs versus just take. Most people do just the opposite, in my experience."

At the time I didn't have any products, other than my business training programs. Tony was instrumental in helping me get into the keynote arena, which was much more inspiring to me than business training.

Giving a keynote, you're up onstage in front of hundreds, if not thousands. Talk about flow and excitement! The energy is palpable. Unfortunately, in many business and corporate training programs, the participants are there because management told them to be there. Many would rather be anywhere else. This is another example of command and control leadership not working; it's a waste of time and money.

At one point, I decided to add business and life coaching to my arsenal. I certainly had the background in both by this time. After all, this was what I did at the AT&T School of Business.

My very first coaching client was done pro bono. Focus on providing value; it will always come back. It may come back from a different source, but it will come back nonetheless.

I worked with an investment advisor from Canada for an entire year. We spoke every single week. At times it was laborious because he had many limiting beliefs and a low self-image to overcome. At the end of that year, however, his income had tripled from when we first began. He literally turned his annual income into a monthly income. I now had a tremendous success story from which to build.

I was then invited to attend a Bob Proctor weekend as his guest. I approached him at the break. We seemed to click instantly, and he apparently saw something in me that he liked. I found another willing business coach and mentor.

Proctor reminded me of my dad in many ways because he was very emotionally closed. He gave me pointers that brought together a lot of the things I had read and studied for years. He took me under his wing. I've told him numerous times how much I appreciate his impact on my life.

A quick fast-forward: Bob was the only person who went into the media in my defense post sweat lodge. Although my lawyers decided not to use him, he even agreed to appear at my mitigation hearing to testify in my defense. The DA spent the better part of four months during trial completely deriding the personal performance industry, and they didn't want to give her a chance to go back down that road. But I owe Bob a tremendous debt of gratitude for his willingness.

Eventually, my feelings regarding keynotes changed. I knew I had more to give than sixty to ninety minutes would allow. I wanted to spend more time with people and dive deeper, giving them skills, techniques, and strategies that would meaningfully address the issues and resistance they were wrestling with. I needed to do something different, and my answer was public events.

## It Always Takes Twice as Long and Costs Twice as Much

Building the business was a long road. I didn't take a salary for ten years. Those who don't know tend to romanticize entrepreneurship, but it's just plain hard. Leading your own business is one of the most difficult challenges you'll ever take on. Yet it can also be the most rewarding.

I poured everything I made back into the company. I was living hand-to-mouth and credit card to credit card. For quite a few years, I ate vision sandwiches and faith cookies. But I knew it was time to be resilient, time to become more resourceful. I told myself, *You must struggle, persevere, and keep the faith.*

*It's in the struggle that potential greatness is born.*

In 2002, I went through an ugly relationship breakup. It all came hurtling down as I simultaneously teetered on the edge of bankruptcy. The 2000 stock market crash had taken its toll. My small portfolio had become even smaller, almost cut in half, and my CPA girlfriend wanted half of everything. I was completely despondent. From a really dark place, I wrote my second book, *Practical Spirituality*.

*Darkness often fuels greatness and creativity for those who will only seize it.*

I typed from pain. I typed from "enough already." It was a catharsis for me to write out my own life lessons and learnings.

I continued to push forward. The dips, struggles, and stalls were many, but when you know where you're going and why you're here, you don't quit. Step by step, with continued effort, perseverance, and grit, I believed I just may have some degree of positive impact on people's lives and businesses.

I had no earthly idea what was still to come.

Yes, I was being built, brick by painful brick, becoming stronger and more resilient. I was gaining confidence, mental toughness, and emotional strength. Had I known the difficulty and pain of what was to come, had I known where my life path was leading me, love it or not, I may have thought much longer and harder about continuing.

I may have had much more hesitation and pause.

**CHAPTER 3**

# FINDING HARMONIC WEALTH

E arly in the 2000s, Jack Canfield, the author of *Chicken Soup for the Soul*, myself, and a few others formed the Transformational Leadership Council (TLC). Our goal was to put together a mastermind group of transformational leaders—brilliant minds who could make a tremendous impact on the world.

Socializing has never been my thing. Networking is more my speed, especially networking with others who share my drive to do something powerful in the world. That was my mindset. But it quickly became apparent that it wasn't the mindset of the majority of the group. Everyone is different, but I believe physical life is far too short not to take advantage of every moment and opportunity to fulfill your purpose.

---

*The problem is, we think we have time. We don't.*

---

Early on, I would make an enormous effort to get to a TLC meeting, and then the group would go on a canoe trip rather than focus on synergizing our skills to create something great. I didn't want to go on a canoe trip. I wanted the group to come together and explore how we were going to change the world. Frankly, if we were not going to change the world, I would rather rest because I was exhausted. I lived on the road over two hundred and fifty days per year. I was on a mission and relentlessly committed to living it and fulfilling it.

---

*If the forces of darkness, disillusionment, and*
*disempowerment are not taking a day off, how can I?*

---

The TLC group met in Vail around 2004-2005, and Australian television producer Rhonda Byrne showed up. She had heard about TLC and had a vision to create a movie based on the law of attraction.

I was intrigued because the law of attraction had always been a part of my programs, albeit a small fraction of the life, business, and leadership principles I was teaching. Ironically, I eventually became well known for this concept, even though it was a minor part compared to the complete scope of my material.

I arrived at the meeting late, flying in from various engagements. Prior to my arrival, Rhonda had made a presentation explaining the idea for the movie. She had talked to the TLC board of directors and wanted all of us to participate and contribute our various perspectives to the film.

When I arrived, they had started filming. I watched my peers go in and out. A long line had formed, and everyone seemed excited. All seemed eager to participate.

Because I was late, I was at the bottom of the list. Finally, my turn came. The person ahead of me came out of the room, and I stepped in. One of Rhonda's staff came over and said, "I'm really sorry, but we've run out of film."

*Are you kidding me?*

With incredible disappointment, I flew back to San Diego thinking, *I guess it wasn't meant to be. Everything happens for a reason.*

Two days later, I got a call at my office from Rhonda Byrne's team. They were going to be in Orange County shooting Mark Victor Hansen, Jack Canfield's partner in the Chicken Soup franchise. Byrne's crew wanted me to drive up from San Diego to shoot my segment on the law of attraction at Mark's office in Orange County.

I drove to Orange County under the expectation that I would probably get fifteen to thirty minutes of film time, as that's what they gave the others in Vail. They shot Mark's segment quickly. I went in, and they ended up filming me for three hours. I was on a roll. Rhonda and her sister were behind the cameras, and we literally laughed, cried, and hugged. It was a great session. Driving back to San Diego, I was pretty high.

More time passed, and Rhonda called me. They had decided to use only a few of the teachers, and I was one of them. Very few people know that the entire project was a labor of love for the content providers. We received no compensation on either the movie or the book.

Rhonda's original vision was to put together a Hollywood movie. She wanted it to be distributed as a feature film. When that didn't work out, she decided to release it on the internet as *The Secret*. At the time, I thought this was a huge mistake.

I was initially disappointed when I viewed *The Secret* for the first time because, in my opinion, my best material ended up on the cutting-room floor. I guess Rhonda, as the producer, didn't feel I focused enough on the law of attraction.

She asked all of us to market it, which we did. Everyone featured in the film had big mail lists, and we all mailed it out like crazy. It went viral.

I was still struggling financially and barely making ends meet. One thing I always made time and found the money for, however, was my own education and study.

## Searching for Inspiration

In November 2005, I took my second trip to Egypt. I had long studied many of the ancient mysteries, and Egypt was, beyond doubt, the epicenter of all Western traditions. On my first trip, I spent more time crawling through temples and tombs than most would ever consider. I meditated between the paws of the Sphinx, and I was granted access to all three chambers of the Great Pyramid. It was just me and me alone, for a full three hours, in this mysterious spiritual landmark. That trip was life-changing.

For this second trip, I decided to spend two weeks in the Sinai desert with the Bedouins, nomadic tribes that herd camels and goats across this vast, barren desert.

I chose to follow the path from Egypt into the Sinai that the children of Israel followed on their exodus. I was also scheduled to climb Mount Sinai and, by special arrangement, spend the entire night alone on top of the mountain in what was said to be Moses' cave. The same cave, the legend states, in which he was inspired to write the Ten Commandments. I was completely thrilled at this opportunity and expected something magical and inspiring to happen.

I desperately needed some inspiration. I was exhausted and tired, working so hard for so long with very little to show in return. Sometimes the greatest tools and training that money, study, and time can afford still seem to fall incredibly short. I'd been at this now for the better part of two decades, and it seemed as if the vision and dream were still too far off to be seen. I was barely hanging on.

I was also scheduled to visit Tell el-Amarna, the ancient city built by one of my long-time heroes, the pharaoh Akhenaten. This also thrilled me and filled me with expectation. Akhenaten was the quintessential visionary, one courageous enough to go against the collective thinking of his day. Something I've always admired.

---

*No one who was normal ever made history.*

---

Akhenaten brought monotheism to the polytheistic Egyptian culture and moved the capital from Cairo to Amarna to honor the one God, Aten, represented by the sun.

Maybe going back to this spiritual epicenter would give me the new inspiration and hope I desperately needed. I was so down and dark that I was considering throwing in the towel. *The Secret* had been filmed, but nothing had happened with it.

The Sinai desert is brutal. Intense heat beats off the sand all day long, and even in the warmest of months, it's extremely cold after dark. As I curled up in my sleeping bag on the sand each night and shivered, my mind drifted to the Bible story of the Israelites being lost in this God-forsaken country for forty years.

Beating sun with no shade and little water by day. Bone-chilling cold by night. And I'm pretty certain they had no down sleeping bags, like the one keeping me semi-warm, in the days of Moses. To leave Egypt with the grand vision of "going to the Promised Land," only to grind and struggle and stall in this barren land for forty years would have taken a mental and emotional toll on even the strongest of spirits—not to mention the physical toll.

I couldn't help but draw metaphoric corollaries to my own life for the last twenty years.

Long a fan of Joseph Campbell and his exhaustive research into world-myth and various spiritual traditions, I was familiar with the common experience found in them all: the hero invariably goes off on his quest fully inspired, only to face incredible odds.

---

*Mythology truly is the history book of the human soul.*

---

## Wadi Maktub

After days of trekking with my Bedouin guide, we arrived at a place in the middle of nowhere that my guide told me was named Wadi Maktub. *Wadi* in Arabic translates as "valley" and *Maktub* as "it is written." The latter word needs a bit more description.

Maktub carries the implication of fate. As in, you can't argue with it, for it's the fate of your life. You can attempt to argue with it, hate it, or resist it. Or you can face it and embrace it. Either way, it's not going to change; it is written.

Wadi Maktub consisted of several large stones, looking completely out of place, smack in the center of the desert. More interesting still were the Arabic and ancient Hebrew inscriptions covering the faces of these rock walls. I had a cursory understanding of the Hebrew alphabet, yet these writings, for the most part, were way too old for me to make out.

Wadi Maktub had a tremendous impact on me. Long sensitive to energy, I could feel the pain in these stone carvings. Maybe it was just a projection of my own pain, but nonetheless I felt a surge of uncontrollable emotions welling up within me.

I asked the guide to interpret what some of these ancients were saying in their carvings, and he said they felt "forsaken by God. Damned. Lost and doomed."

I lost it.

Sobs rolled out of me, and tears streamed down my face. I bent over and put my hands on my knees, feebly trying to control what was not to be controlled. I continued my downward bend until I buckled at the knees and just knelt in the desert and sobbed.

I cried and cried until I had no more to give. I was in the Valley of Fate, and I knew beyond a doubt that this was my fate as well. It was written. These feelings. These doubts. These thoughts of being completely forsaken. It was fate and not to be argued with.

Little did I know that in just four short years I would feel these feelings in multiples of tens.

My guide said nothing, and we never spoke about it. I can only imagine what may have been running through his mind.

By the time we arrived at Mount Sinai, my physical exhaustion from long periods in the desert nearly matched my spiritual and emotional exhaustion. I felt I was reliving an ancient metaphor, to say the least.

We stayed for the first time in many nights in a hotel at the base of the mountain. It was beyond rustic, but after days in the desert, a soft bed, warm shower, and four walls felt like the ultimate luxury. I could see Mount Sinai outside my window. We were scheduled to climb to the peak the next morning.

I awakened the next morning knowing the task at hand, yet I was still tired and uninspired. The previous week in the desert and the impact of Wadi Maktub made calling it quits seem all the more attractive and viable.

At 7,500 feet, Sinai is a moderately high mountain. Yet coming from sea level and already being in a state of exhaustion, the trek was tough. My guide, who was used to the climb, was moving way too fast for my liking, and I was getting angry.

---

*Once your mind gets in a downward spiral,*
*you're quickly circling the mental/emotional drain.*

---

Every fiber in my body and soul wanted to quit—literally as well as figuratively. *Why the hell did I decide to trek in the desert and climb a mountain at this point in my flailing career? What had I hoped to get from more work? Wouldn't it have been much smarter to go somewhere and relax and recuperate? Why is life so hard? I know I have a lot to share, so why hasn't the world realized it yet?*

Obviously, none of this self-questioning served to support and inspire me. Quite the contrary. It was doing the exact opposite.

I continued to climb.

Reflecting on my climb up Salcantay in Peru, I remembered this feeling well. Muscles cramping. Self-talk screaming. But what do you do?

You continue to climb.

Such is life.

To get up day after day, week after week, month after month, year after year, decade after decade—over the course of a lifetime—and forge ahead against the obstacles we face is the greatest victory of all. We must always remember that the only time we're truly defeated is when we give up. Not until.

---

*The greatest victory a leader can experience is the victory over self.*

---

I realized that life is never in perfect balance and equilibrium. In fact, walking the tightrope of life is a constant state of being out of balance yet compensating to stay on the wire.

When you watch any tightrope artist, they're constantly swaying back and forth, adjusting and readjusting, yet they keep moving. To stop and stay static only amplifies the problem.

The term "harmony" came to mind and expressed this dynamism much more clearly.

---

*A symphony is not in balance. It's in harmony.*

---

A symphony sometimes leads with the bass, sometimes the horns, then the woodwinds, then the drums. All come together in perfect rhythm and timing, in their perfect time and place, to create a masterpiece. Such is life.

Sometimes you're working on your finances and business, so you're not spending as much time with your family or in the gym. This is realistic. It's a fact. But you don't totally disregard family or gym. That's when you'll break and cause even more problems. The tightrope walker doesn't throw down his pole, rather, he constantly dips it this way and that in perfect rhythm to the beat of the dance.

Harmonic Wealth® was born in this moment on the side of Mount Sinai. I had long known that when you trace the root of the word "wealth" back to its origins, it translates as well-being. Harmony and well-being. Wasn't that what we're all ultimately seeking? Particularly in the midst of a storm?

I continued to climb with my tired, cramping legs.

I reached the top of the mountain and, given my previous arrangements, was granted access to stay there for the night. I huddled in a very small cave in which, legend has it, the mighty Ten Commandments were penned. I was full of anticipation to be infused with tremendous inspiration and insight.

I remembered the countless times I had heard the story in Sunday school regarding God telling Moses to take off his shoes because he was on holy ground. I had promised myself to do the same. The unconscious mind loves ritual, and I was prepared to give mine a full-on ritualistic experience. I had prepared mentally for this moment and visualized it for months.

But I was still exhausted.

The mental and emotional toll had taken about everything I had. There I was, huddled in a cave with nothing but a small candle in the pitch black of night. To make matters worse, it was freezing cold!

The other promise I had made to myself, besides removing my shoes, was to stay awake the entire night. I mean, how many times in life do you get this type of opportunity? I was in Moses' cave—the man who led the Israelites out of Egypt and changed the course of history. This was an opportunity any leader would dream of. You can sleep any other time.

As I sat there sleepy and shivering, even in my down parka, I came up with a variety of reasons why it would be completely stupid to remove my shoes, and the stupid reasons were all logical: *Who said you have to remove your shoes anyway? You well know, James, that even the Hasidic Jews tell you that the Old Testament is allegory and metaphor, not to be taken literally. They penned it! Do you think that taking your shoes off in this pitch black, cramped, and frigid cave is really going to do something spiritual for you? Come on. Seriously. You're exhausted. Mentally and emotionally taxed. The last thing you need is to catch the flu.*

The internal dialogue continued to scream as I slowly unlaced my hiking boots. I learned long ago that you have to be willing to sacrifice for your outcomes. Sometimes you have to become literally obsessed with your outcomes. Be willing to give every last thing you have—even when it's hard, *most often* when it's hard. The prize always has a price.

We tend to forget that the original meaning of the word "sacrifice" translates as "to make sacred." In the traditions, when a sacrifice is made to God, it's given up fully and completely. Some gave their most prized possessions. The story of the prophet Abraham maintains he was willing to sacrifice his only son.

---

*Sometimes the greatest things we can give are our small desires and comforts for something much greater, bigger, and vastly grander than those things.*

---

In the actual sacrifice, no matter how silly or illogical, we are telling ourselves—as well as the entire universe, call it God—we're committed to something beyond our own comfort and small ego desires.

The cold night air was a shock to my bare feet, and the one small candle provided little warmth. And so the all-night vigil began. I wrote page after page in my journal, just a free flow of consciousness and too much to share here. But it centered on the illusions so many of us face and struggle with regarding how life *should be* versus how it really is.

While it's important to appreciate and celebrate the peaks we summit, life is not about arriving at some magnificent summit or resting there to enjoy the view. For the majesty of a mountain is only as majestic as its contrast to the depth of the valley and the emptiness of the sky it stands against.

Without the depth of the valley and the emptiness of the sky, we see no majesty. It's much like the dips and dives and dances of the symphony. Without the space between the notes, the pauses, the crescendos followed by the diminuendos, we hear no tension, drama, or color.

The false expectation of "perfect balance" that's so long been propagated and bought into, either consciously or unconsciously, has created a lack of fulfilment or zest for life itself. In pursing the far-off fantasy of arriving in that perfect place where it all falls perfectly into place, we lose our life.

In quantum physics, every positron with a positive charge has a corresponding electron with a negative charge. Positive and negative always come in equal pairs. It cannot be otherwise.

Wasn't it my pain and suffering over the last two weeks that made this accomplishment so grand? Isn't it what I'm still writing about today, all these years later? If a helicopter had flown me into Wadi Maktub and then dropped me on top of Mount Sinai, would the memory and victory be the same?

Of course not. Would you even be reading the story had it unfolded that way? I think we both know the answer.

I heard shuffling outside the cave that startled me out of my deep internal trance. I had been staring at the one flickering candle for hours, and it was nearly burned away. Unbeknown to me, a morning ritual was about to unfold. I was shocked to realize it was almost dawn. No one was aware of me being huddled down in this subterranean cave. I slowly stuck my head out to see people lining up and facing eastward, the direction of the rising sun and new birth in the traditions.

As the sun began its slow ascent, these people started singing: "Let there be peace on earth, and let it begin with me." People from all over the world in their own native tongue. Man, could I ever relate to that sentiment! Tears flowed once again.

I would later find out that it's customary for people to begin the trek around midnight and climb for three to four hours in the darkness to meet the dawn.

It was beautiful. All these people from all over the world singing, and me crawling cold and stiff from Moses' cave—now my cave as well. I could not have imagined a more perfect capper on the topic of harmony had I written the script myself. Maybe at some level I did.

I had ascended the mountain tired and frustrated, and I descended revitalized and reborn. I was still physically tired—exhausted actually, with no sleep—but I was also suddenly revitalized, inspired, and, dare I say, harmonious inside.

For I now realized that true harmony, like wealth, is not money. Not ease. Not comfort. True well-being is being in love with life, both the ups and the downs. For what are the peaks without the pits?

## Life After the Abyss

---

*"Being an entrepreneur is like eating broken glass and staring into the abyss of death."*
**—Elon Musk**

---

I had been ready to throw in the towel, and now once again I was ready to push forward, fresh and renewed. Little did I know what was brewing just below the surface. Do we ever?

One day just a few weeks after my return, my office received a call from Larry King's producer, Wendy Walker. Appearing on *Larry King Live* was so far beyond my comprehension I couldn't even get my head around it: *I am going on Larry King?*

After the segment aired, my website got so much traffic in a single hour that the server crashed. After that, everything happened fast. By this time, I was doing morning shows in every city I was in because it would help fill the room for later that night. I was on the road nonstop. Crack-of-dawn pickup every Monday morning, three to four appearances in three to four cities per week, home late Friday night, work all weekend to catch up, and out again Monday morning.

After *Larry King Live*, the phones rang off the hook. Napoleon Hill said, back in the 1950s, there's a big difference between wishing for something and being prepared to receive it. I had wished for this for a long, long time, but frankly, I was not even close to being prepared when it happened.

I had to hire additional team members. Potential clients were getting busy signals when calling my office, so I had to get a new phone system with many more lines. I had to find a new office space to house the team members because we were maxed out in the tiny office we occupied. I was spending all kinds of money in anticipation of future opportunity—money I didn't have.

The standing joke for my team and those who know me is that when the floodgates open and you must figure out a way to plug the dam, those are "high-level problems to have." High-level problems beat the hell out of low-level problems. You want them, even though they're like chewing on broken glass sometimes.

The bane of every leader and entrepreneur is that you must be able to dance with long-term opportunity while effectively tending to short-term needs. Damn, there's that harmony dance again. I was maneuvering my pole, swaying back and forth, and doing my best to stay on the shaky wire.

Long-term and short-term are both important. If you look only at one versus the other, you go down. It's a delicate dance. I leased new office space, we moved in, and we had everything up and running.

I was sitting in my office one day, and my executive assistant comes running in and says, "You are not going to believe who I've got on the phone."

I said, "Bill Clinton?" This was always a standing joke as well.

She said, "Oprah Winfrey!" It wasn't literally Oprah, but it was her producer.

*Are you kidding me?*

I can't tell you how long I had visualized being on *Oprah*. So much so that I used to watch Oprah's show pretending that I was sitting on the couch next to her. She would ask questions, and I would pretend she was asking me. I would answer her in my mind.

When I arrived in Chicago for the taping, I was running on pure adrenaline. When the show started, Rhonda Byrne was interviewed by herself first, and then they went to a break. In the next segment, they brought in those of us who were featured in the film and ushered us into the front row of the audience— Jack Canfield, Michael Beckwith, Lisa Nichols, and me. The audience roared thunderously. It was completely surreal.

Beckwith was sitting to my right, and he leaned over and said, "Hey, dude, we're on *Oprah*."

"Yes, we are," I responded with a grin.

I was in a much better position to handle what was about to come down the road this time. During the first week after I was on *Oprah*, we did over $300,000 in product sales on the website.

Two weeks after the first show, we got another call from Oprah's producer: "She wants you and Michael Beckwith to come back." The two of us did the show again, and we were invited to a meeting with her after the taping.

Oprah wanted to contract with us to be on her show once, maybe twice a month. Not only that, she was going to turn the stage over to us completely. She painted a very enticing picture and dropped Dr. Phil's name into the conversation more than a couple times. She obviously made Phil's career. Oprah's a good salesperson and a good businesswoman, and she knows what she's doing.

By this time, my company was off and running. We were doing well. I had retained an agent, John Ferriter, from William Morris. He was helping negotiate the contracts with Oprah. At the same time, the producers from Larry King's show were talking to Beckwith and me about putting together our own show for Telepictures. Then Ellen DeGeneres came into the mix.

As much as I was interested in having my own show, Telepictures was going up against the queen of transformational television—Oprah *is*

Oprah, after all. We waited through a lot of chess moves back and forth and a lot of contention between the parties competing for our presence and expertise.

My agent John was fielding all of this. The producers for Telepictures scheduled us to fly in to meet Ellen for dinner on Thanksgiving eve. As fate would have it, Oprah called and wanted us on her show again at the very same time as the Ellen dinner. At the end of the day, Oprah won out. The producers who were pitching Ellen were furious with us, and, unfortunately, that broke the relationship.

It upset me. I really wanted to meet Ellen and would love to have danced with her on her show. I guess it wasn't meant to be. Not yet anyway.

I was scheduled to do an evening event prior to this second *Oprah* appearance. I couldn't do a commercial flight from where I was in time to make it to Chicago for the taping, so Oprah chartered a plane. I flew the entire night on her chartered plane and didn't get a hint of sleep. If I thought I looked tired the first time, I looked like I'd had a week of sleep compared to what I looked like this second time.

I finished her show, made a mad dash for the exit, and rushed back to the airport to grab another plane. I appeared on Oprah's show in the afternoon and led an event in a different city that very same night.

---

*"Success is hard. If you don't love it,*
*you'll quit like any sane person would."*
**—Steve Jobs**

---

We had Oprah's contract in front of us. It was comprehensive and a big commitment on my part, with no guarantee that she would ever use me or continue to use me. My agent posed this question, "What happens, James, if you sign this contract and she no longer wants you?"

The contract would still be in effect.

The risk here was enormous. I had a thirty-three-person team and their families depending on me to make the best decisions for the company and for them. This is a big weight to bear.

I really wanted to work with Oprah. Who wouldn't? I pondered and labored and prayed. I did everything within my power to convince myself that this was the right thing to do. At the end of the day, I had to make what I believed to be the most solid decision for my business and my team. Remember, leaders must make decisions, even if they're hard and uncomfortable.

When you grow your company to the level that people are depending on you, you don't have the luxury to roll the dice irresponsibly, even if the payoff might be huge. Yes, you must take calculated risk. But irresponsible risk? When every fiber of your intuition tells you otherwise? No.

---

*We don't need more data. What we need is more intuition and action.*

---

It was during the taping of one of Oprah's shows that I publicly used the phrase Harmonic Wealth for the first time.

During one of the Q&A sessions with the audience, I responded to a question, "What you need, what you really want in your life, is Harmonic Wealth. As I define it, this is a state of harmony and well-being in the five key areas of life: financial, relational, mental, physical, and spiritual."

Oprah stopped me and said, "Wait a second. Say that again."

I said it again, and she followed with, "That's the title of a book!"

I said, "Yes, it is."

After these appearances on *Oprah*, people were flocking to my events. It was a whirlwind, the coming to fruition of the film *The Secret* and the whole buzz that followed.

The second time I was on *Larry King Live*, I couldn't make it to the studio. The producer, Wendy Walker, flew the camera crew to Phoenix and broadcast me live from an event where I had twelve hundred people in the room.

When I first signed on with my agent, John Ferriter, he said to me, "You need to write a book."

I had been thinking about writing a book and told John I wanted it to come out early that next year. This was right when *The Secret* was reaching the peak of its success. John introduced me to Andy McNichol, their publicist at William Morris, who informed me that the book wasn't coming out next year, it was coming out *now*.

I was on the road again nonstop, three or four cities a week, at least twelve cities per month—every single month. I would get offstage, go back to my room, and burn the midnight oil going through scripts and transcripts, reading them, tweaking them, and turning them into a manuscript. It was a grind. I was constantly running on four hours of sleep.

When *Harmonic Wealth* came out and hit the *New York Times* bestseller list, I was elated. I was on *The Today Show* to promote it just after it was released. Subsequently, I stepped into a bookstore in Manhattan and saw my book lining the walls. I can't tell you how great that felt. Surreal. Later, I had to catch a plane, and as I passed the airport bookstore, I saw my book front and center, displayed on a table. Absolutely surreal.

What I didn't realize at the time was how monumental my book would become in my own life, how the lessons of *Harmonic Wealth* would eventually save my sanity and my life.

## Less than Zero

After the trial and prison, I was literally left with nothing. Everything I had worked for decades to build, my entire empire, was gone in the blink of an eye—except I wasn't just left with zero. I was left with less than zero.

I had lost my home, my business, my car, every worldly possession, and every penny I worked so hard to earn. Not only that, I was $20 million in debt. When you're $20 million in the red, zero starts to look pretty damn good. From where I stood, "broke" was a long climb up.

*Money is a myth, a myth that must be understood and unraveled if you choose to live any kind of a fulfilling life.*

We've all been conditioned to think that money means something. But the truth is, money means nothing beyond the meaning you apply to it. The vast majority of us are attributing meaning to something that inherently has no meaning at all.

Why? Because we've been led to believe that if we only have more money, our lives will be better, easier, and more fulfilling. Trust me, they won't. Therein lies the core of the money myth.

---

*Your true wealth is not what you have. True wealth is what you're left with when all you have is gone.*

---

One of the main things that saved me when I walked out of the penitentiary, with literally less than nothing, was that I had already understood and broken the money myth in my own mind. I already knew that my true wealth wasn't what I had, it was what I had left when all the material things were gone. While it *appeared* I had nothing, I was actually wealthy beyond belief. In fact, wealthier than I'd ever been in my life!

Don't get me wrong—losing everything I had put my entire life into for over two decades was beyond devastating. Emerging back into the world and starting from less than zero at fifty-five was overwhelming and daunting. But if my life had been all about the money and the things, I would *never* have made it through.

Fortunately, my life was about much more than that.

How did I make it through? Mental Wealth. I had developed and refined my own mental mastery, mental toughness, and emotional strength to keep focused, even when the storm was crashing and rolling all around me. I got myself up daily and fought The Resistance (the great foe that attempts to hold us back and keep us limited and stuck) that raged both inside and out.

I had Spiritual Wealth and emotional strength and the fortitude to find a higher purpose and meaning in the chaos and loss.

I had Relational Wealth, first and foremost with myself. I knew who I was, despite the accusations, lack of understanding, hate, crucifixion, and vilification in the media and on the internet.

I had Physical Wealth, a strong and healthy body and heart. I had the fortitude and grit to keep going, even when I didn't feel like it, which, honestly, was most days—especially in prison.

I no longer had Financial Wealth, but the qualities which created it remained and propelled me ahead.

This is where far too many people get overpowered by the myth of money. The only type of wealth that can be taken away from you without your control is Financial Wealth. All the other types are yours, and no one can take them away. Unless you let them, that is.

The bad news is, every one of us can lose our material wealth at a moment's notice. You never know what lies in wait just around the corner. The big black truck eventually pulls up in front of every business and every home. I didn't expect it. I never would have dreamt it.

The difference is, I was prepared. Are you?

## CHAPTER 4

# SPIRITUAL WARRIOR

A fter the success of *Harmonic Wealth*, I continued to do the free public events and my whole seminar series—eleven unique and distinct events, ranging from two to five days each. Normally, I'd put in sixteen-hour days. These events were content rich and transformative, but the schedule became increasingly challenging. Every blessing is a curse, and every coin has two sides. I got more media exposure and more notoriety. Therefore, I had less and less privacy, and for a guy who is very private and naturally introverted, this was difficult. I had to wrestle my own internal demons because I'm not the kind of person who needs a lot of social interaction.

If I'm not teaching, I'd just as soon be curled up by myself with a good book or a movie that makes me think and teaches something. Yet it was my time in the spotlight. I didn't complain. After all, I created it. I'd be rushing through an airport, and people would stop me, saying, "Oh my God. You're James Arthur Ray."

"Yes."

"Can I take a quick photo?"

"Well, you know, I'm running late for this plane."

Yet I knew if I said no, they'd think I was aloof or didn't care. I can only imagine how some celebrities may feel, and they're not even in an industry professing to help people. When you're in an industry that is centered on helping and caring, how can you say no?

I was constantly in a wrestling match with my own internal demons: *I asked for this, so I can't be upset about it. Be grateful, James. Be grateful.*

It's always perplexing to me when I hear celebrities complain about wanting to be left alone or when I see them get angry and lash out at photographers and fans. I get it. Truly I do. But who created it? Who asked for it?

Absolute responsibility resided in one pair of shoes: my own.

I was constantly on, and it was becoming more and more exhausting. It was starting to take a physical, mental, and emotional toll on me. One of my team members said to me backstage at an event, "James, there's no way in hell you can go on."

I would be backstage, lying on the floor, with pain shooting through my back and my feet on fire. As mentioned, I often held events that consisted of sixteen-hour days for two to five days straight. I just had so much content and value I wanted to provide.

Then I'd hear the music start. I'd sit up, take a deep breath, put on a big smile, bounce up and down a few times, and *BAM!* I'm on.

By this time, I had professional security with me at all times. I always had two security guards, not because I thought I was going to get hurt, but when you start having one thousand or two thousand people in one room, you're going to get some unique individuals who might do something dangerous or strange.

At one particular Harmonic Wealth Weekend, within the first thirty minutes of a two-day experience, I jumped off my stool and something in my knee popped. My knee buckled, and I nearly passed out. My head was spinning, and I started perspiring profusely. I remembered the corporate trainer's motto I had learned many years before at AT&T: "When in doubt, breakout."

This referenced the fact that at times, as a trainer or seminar leader, you're not sure what to do next. Breakout sessions within the audience (putting them to a task) always gives you time to collect your thoughts and assess the situation.

I put the participants into a quick exercise I made up on the spot and went backstage. I always had an elevated stage, normally 4 feet high. As I attempted to go down the stairs behind the curtain to figure out what happened, I crumpled on the stairs. I had torn a ligament in the back of my knee, and I literally could not walk.

The security guards—two big, strapping guys—had to carry me back up the stairs and set me onstage. I was in unbearable pain the entire weekend. With a soaring temperature, I was shivering and drenched in cold perspiration, but I had to deliver.

What do you say to people who come from all over the world to see you? "I'm sorry. I hurt myself. I can't do this." No. You deliver. The show must go on. It was excruciating, but I gave it everything I had.

Maintaining this kind of schedule took an enormous toll. I told my team members, "Something has to change. We have to figure out a way to scale this business so it's not all on my shoulders."

One of the great challenges of every entrepreneur is that 99 percent of the time, we get into our line of business because we're good at what we do. At some point, however, if you're fortunate enough to have your business grow, you must change roles.

You have to move from technician to leader. In other words, you must stop doing what you're good at, duplicate yourself, and then work *on* your business instead of *in* your business. This is a very difficult shift for most because we invariably think that "no one can do it like me." In many cases, this is true.

---

*You must let go if you want to continue to grow.*

---

Ask yourself, *Would I rather give great value to a larger amount of people or continue to give masterful value to a small amount of people? Which will make the biggest impact?*

## Entrepreneurial Challenges

We hired a new team member to train potential trainers, selected from top clients and graduates who were interested to deliver my material. My strategy was that, at some point, I would stop doing the free events and the trainers would take them over. I had a coaching certification program as well, and little by little I was attempting to scale the model and content. But I wasn't moving fast enough, and in the meantime it was all still 100 percent on me.

Overhead had crept up to $500,000 a month, just to make payroll and pay the bills—$6 million a year before I personally made a single dollar. That's a heavy load for any one person to carry.

However, the biggest expenditure was not payroll. Some of my events cost a quarter of a million dollars to produce, especially the five-day events, because I never spared any sparkle or sizzle.

The experiences in my early years of going to rock concerts and watching my favorite bands perform were being incorporated into the content. We were masterful at using music to accelerate emotional states of experience.

My financial advisor said to me at one point, "James, you have to cut this back. Your margins are really tight." But it had never been about margins for me—not that they weren't important. Of course they were.

*If there's no margin, then ultimately there's no mission.*

But the primary driver for me was always client experience and value received. I know from my background in behavioral sciences and psychology that if you can get someone emotionally involved first, they're more likely to open up intellectually.

People love the lights, the visuals, the hugging and back-rubs, the dancing and the music. They would say to themselves, "It's a big party"—a leadership, personal performance, and transformation party. All this fun and growth came without the deleterious effects of normal partying.

Yet as I pondered profit and loss and all the numbers continuously, I asked myself, *If the production all goes away, will they continue to stay and learn? Do they want to grow and absorb the content? Or do they just want to be entertained?*

I hoped that education and growth was a high value, but I wasn't 100 percent sure, and I had a business to run and team members and their families depending on me. How could I risk taking that chance?

I couldn't.

But life was about to make the decision for me and bring it all to a screeching halt.

## Running on Empty

The entire economy and real estate market went sideways in 2008, so event ticket sales plummeted and my company, James Ray International, was deeply in the red. I had personally loaned the company $1.2 million of my own money to keep the doors open and to make payroll.

From 2006 to the beginning of 2008, I was making between $2 million and $4 million a year in bonuses because we were doing extremely well; the company was turning a profit. But at the end of 2008, I stopped taking a salary once again because we were scrambling hard. I thought, *Here we go again. Welcome to the world of the entrepreneur.*

The company was basically insolvent. Not only did I have the financial pressures of keeping the ship afloat, but I was also physically and emotionally exhausted.

I had a high-level mastermind group called the World Wealth Society, which consisted of an inner circle of individuals each investing $60,000 a year to be a member and have access to special opportunities not available to non-members. With monthly overhead having crept up, even this income didn't provide much run rate.

I took seventy-five WWS members to Egypt in 2008. I was miserable the entire trip. I owed these members my presence, my time, and 100 percent of my energy, but I was mentally and emotionally out of gas, drained from all the years of running from one city to the next, and tapped out from the recent financial struggles.

At the same time, I'd invested $650,000 in an infomercial to introduce a larger audience to the concepts of Harmonic Wealth. Timing could not have been worse. With the economy in the tank and the real estate crisis, people wanted financial wealth, not harmonic. They only cared about saving themselves and paying the bills. While harmony was the antidote, it was a near impossible sale, given the mass-mindset of mass-hysteria.

Television time slots are expensive, and we were purchasing large blocks of these slots to run the infomercial. I had not heard a word from my producer and ad buyer since I went to Egypt. Not a good sign.

I remember calling him from this ancient land: "Hey, I haven't heard from you. How is the infomercial doing?"

"Well, it's not doing as well as we would like."

This nebulous answer told me it was doing terrible, so he was dodging and dancing. It was his job to make it work. My company paid their company big dollars not only to produce this but to make it profitable.

We were not only buying expensive ad spots, but we had also hired a telemarketing firm to field the incoming calls from those spots.

"What specifically does 'not doing as well as we would like' mean?"

"Well," he said hesitantly, "we've sold thirty-five units and had seventeen returns."

"You've got to be kidding me!"

"I think we just need a little more time to dial it in."

"Pull it."

"Now, wait, James. You have a lot invested in this. I suggest we give it more time."

Of course he did. My company was funding the entire project, and they had a piece of the results on the backend. They'd made their money on the $650,000, but they wanted additional bonuses and commissions. In fact, they were counting on them. They probably budgeted for them. On my dime!

"Pull it! Right now!"

I was devastated.

Leadership is about taking risk, taking big bold action. I had done so, and I put this project into play long before anyone knew about (other than the government and banks, who were completely asleep at the wheel) or could have predicted the collapse.

Sometimes, as a leader, you must be willing to "kill your own baby." Believe me, it's not easy. But the market conditions were clearly telling me this was *not* going to work.

Time to cut and move.

## The Experience

In 2009 I took fifty-five WWS members to Peru with me. Just two weeks back from Peru, I was on my way to Sedona for my five-day Spiritual Warrior event— the most demanding program we conducted for me personally. It was a small group of people, and they all had direct access to me. Twenty-four hours a day for five days nonstop.

The entire week was centered on people doing "spiritual war" with their own demons and unresolved emotional issues and trauma. Most of these issues came from childhood. We all have them. The emotional toll that level of catharsis took on me with fifty-five people emoting for five days and coming to me for answers was difficult beyond description.

We had conducted the Spiritual Warrior event several times at the Angel Valley Ranch, a 70-acre remote desert retreat center outside Sedona, Arizona. The program always concluded with a sweat lodge held on the final evening, immediately prior to a celebratory graduation dinner. This was the final breakthrough celebration for each participant after a grueling week of digging into their own emotional baggage.

The participants arrived Saturday evening, October 3, 2009, and the event continued through Friday morning, October 9. Each attendee signed a comprehensive release form when they registered for the event acknowledging that the exercises were physically challenging and completely voluntary, and also that they were completely responsible for themselves.

The release also stated that there were potential health risks, up to and including death. Furthermore, it informed them that advice from a physician should be obtained prior to the event, and that neither I nor my company would be held liable for any pre-existing medical condition, nor any unforeseen, but pre-advised, potential outcome.

I hired one of the best law firms in California, Greenberg & Glusker, to draw up these "rock solid" releases of liability and full personal responsibility forms. I really thought they meant something. Little did I know.

The Spiritual Warrior event allowed attendees to undertake a spiritual journey identifying the beliefs and behaviors that were holding them back from achieving their personal and business goals. It required the participants to identify the goal they wanted to reach, and then to uncover and articulate any obstacles in the way of achieving that goal. Then, through a series of exercises I facilitated, the participants would let go of the limiting factors, mostly through acceptance, forgiving, and finding what their difficulties and challenges had taught them, so they could move forward in an empowered way toward what they chose to accomplish.

The first evening of Spiritual Warrior culminated in a hair-buzzing ceremony. This was similar to the haircuts received in the military or upon entering a Buddhist monastery. The press would later spin it into a "head shaving," which conjures up razors and nothing left but skin. No one *shaved* their head. Many buzzed their hair with clippers, but no one "shaved." And like everything else during the week, it was completely voluntary.

The purpose for buzzing was a physical metaphor, symbolic of a new beginning. It allowed the participants to demonstrate their commitment to transforming their life, even when uncomfortable, and to make a public commitment to this through the symbolic act of buzz cutting their hair and letting go.

I encouraged the participants to fully engage in this and all processes—I called this "playing full-on."

Sweat lodge is a big part of the shamanic traditions and is found in many cultures, going all the way back to the Greco-Roman era if not even earlier. I studied with a shaman in the Andes for a couple of years. I also attended Native American events and studied different shamanic modalities from other cultures. Hence, I knew the power of experiential learning and had long utilized various modalities and means.

In the tradition, you go into a small womb-like space that's dark and tight and emerge symbolically reborn. While this sounds intense, it's far from uncommon. Christianity is replete with references to dying to the old self. In fact, St. Peter stated, "I die daily."

Obviously "being reborn" is not a literal physical death in the case of St. Peter, in Christianity, nor in the lodge. Rather a letting go and releasing of old thoughts, beliefs, habits, and limitations and leaving them behind. Letting them "die," if you will. Mentally and emotionally you resolve to let those things go, and you leave them as you exit the lodge.

You could have this same resolve at some level just getting up from a chair and exiting a room if you made a definite decision to do so. The added value of the lodge, and other experiential learning situations, is that you must struggle with your own internal dialogue and physical limitations within the experience itself. Just as in business and, most importantly, life.

---

*Change is hard. That's why most never do it.*

---

A true leader is equal parts Warrior, Leader, and Sage.

Very simply put, Warrior is grit, stamina, endurance, courage, and self-sacrifice. Leader is intelligence, meaning, cause, and purpose. Sage is heart, spiritual connectivity, wisdom, and love.

Business is for Warriors and Gladiators. Period. In life, you must walk your own path and follow your own purpose. You must know and live your own highest values and virtues. This was one of the main goals for the participants of the Spiritual Warrior program. Each person had their own personal needs and goals. Each was on a mission to tackle their inner demons and release and strengthen the inner Warrior.

As the release form advised, the lodge is hot. It's uncomfortable. It's tight and cramped. Personally, I wasn't overly fond of the lodge. Anyone who knows me at all knows that I'm really averse to heat. I always tend to run hot. Because I had to run the lodge and be in there for the entire eight to twelve rounds, I often trained in the weeks prior in a sauna to ramp up.

At the Spiritual Warrior event the sweat lodge was the sizzle, not the steak. The steak was the breakthrough that people experienced both mentally and emotionally during the exercises of the week. I did other experiential learning exercises at other events. Things like fire walks, arrow breaks, rebar bends, board breaks, glass walks, and rope courses.

I knew the power of facing your fear and overcoming it.

A transference happens when a person recognizes, *If I did that thing, I can now do this other thing.* I always added experiential learning exercises to the live events to illustrate the power of moving past limitations, to put some experiential sizzle on the content, and to facilitate integration and transference to daily business and life.

The sweat lodge was a great way to end the Spiritual Warrior event, but it was tough. It's hot as hell in a sweat lodge. You wrestle with the dilemma: *Am I going to succumb to my smaller self-desires and comforts and get out of here? Or am I going to push through?*

This was a struggle I knew all too well. Experience proves that every entrepreneur does. We all consider quitting. Throwing in the towel and giving up. The strongest decide to continue and conquer instead of quit.

---

*Mental toughness and emotional strength are the two most important qualities you can develop.*

---

These are the traits the sweat lodge was designed to inspire.

### Construction of the Lodge

The lodge itself was built by the staff at Angel Valley Ranch using willow branches and twigs scavenged from the property and soaked in a nearby creek to make them supple. As part of my rental agreement with the retreat center, their employees and vendors constructed the lodge and provided a fire keeper and several other supervisory personnel who were on-hand during the experience.

The lodge was framed by a wooden structure called the kiva, originally built in 2008 by David Singing Bear, a Native American who had extensive experience building sweat lodge structures. He was assisted by Ted and Debbie Mercer, part of the team provided by Angel Valley Ranch, who were the builders as well as the fire keepers for my ceremony in October. The sweat lodge area was encircled by rocks intended to define the sacred space. In the traditions, a sweat lodge is similar to going into a temple, mosque, or synagogue.

As the Angel Valley team built the kiva, many of the Native American spiritual practices were observed under Singing Bear's supervision. In each hole that was dug in the ground to create the foundation, an offering was made and a blessing was given by each of those hired by Angel Valley to assist.

Singing Bear also instructed the helpers to hang prayer beads on the wooden support sticks inside, outside, and near the door to the kiva, which were left there permanently. Once the kiva was complete, it became a permanent structure on the property. Singing Bear left the ranch—his job was complete.

When a sweat lodge is to be conducted on the property, the kiva is covered with a variety of blankets, old sleeping bags, tarps, and various other items of thick fabric. The blankets are layered on the kiva to eliminate the possibility of light coming in and to maximize the steam and the heat contained within the lodge once the experience is underway. When the layers of blankets are in place, they're covered with tarps, then the entire structure is covered with a large brown rubber covering.

This entire process was completed prior to my or any of my team's arrival.

An adult couldn't stand up in the finished structure—it was about 4 feet tall at its apex. When the lodge is fully assembled, there's one opening for inflow and outflow which is quite low to the ground, requiring the lodge participants to squat down and duck or crawl in order to enter or exit.

The only other way to exit the sweat lodge is to lift one of the sides off the ground and slide under the layer of tarps and blankets. None of the blankets or tarps were secured in any way. They just lay across the dome structure freely.

Next to the lodge structure a fire pit is constructed. Lava rocks, called "grandfathers," are gathered from the Angel Valley Ranch property and heated in the fire pit. Once the stones have been gathered, they're blessed and given an offering of tobacco and sage. A prayer is recited so the stones are as energetically pure as possible. The fire is stoked constantly so that the stones maintain the brilliant red glow that comes with the heat created in this earthen oven.

## The Sweat Lodge Experience

As you can tell, the whole setup is very ritualistic and detailed. If you've ever been to a Catholic Mass you've experienced similar things with incense, prayers, chanting, sitting, standing, and repeating. This was no different. Much pomp and circumstance.

All of this was conducted under the supervision of Angel Valley and apart from any participation from my team. That was one of the major things they were paid to do. While the lodge is in progress, the fire keeper monitors the heating of the stones. The door keeper stands next to the door of the lodge and is charged with "holding the energy of the fire." This is a type of internal prayer or visualization to constantly project good intentions.

The sweat lodge experience is held in rounds. A round generally lasts from eight to twelve minutes. After each round, some participants exit the lodge and go to a comfort station. The comfort station is supplied with electrolyte water, lemon water, Gatorade, cut fruit, and towels. The ranch team is also on-hand with hoses to spray water on any of the participants who want a deeper cool-down.

On the afternoon of Thursday, October 8, 2009, all the Spiritual Warrior participants were celebrating what they had accomplished during the week. They felt lighter because they were dropping emotional baggage long carried. That day, a couple of hours prior, as we prepared to go to the sweat lodge, everybody was hugging and crying and high-fiving each other. They were at a peak, a fever pitch, and proud of themselves.

*I've thought numerous times—if I had just stopped right there . . .*

We had requested that one hundred stones be assembled for the fire pit. Unbeknown to me, the Angel Valley Ranch team decided that day to build the fire base using logs from a wood pile consisting of construction debris. This was uncommon—and very dangerous.

## Build-up to Tragedy

When Ted Mercer built the fire that October day, he would later testify in the trial that "he used the wood stacked next to the pit—some of it pressure-treated construction wood." A quick internet search describes the toxicity and danger of burning pressure-treated wood. You never do this. It can be deadly.

Before the experience began, Ted Mercer pulled me aside and told me that the fire was the hottest he had ever built and that the stones were the hottest he had ever experienced. Before we entered the lodge, I had him repeat this disclosure to the participants.

There's a recording of me describing the environment prior to the sweat lodge experience and informing them they may feel like they were going to die, but they would not.

I truly believed this.

I told them there were volunteers, all of whom had attended the Spiritual Warrior event at least once before, inside the lodge stationed at the north, south, east, and west to help them during the lodge experience if they required support or assistance. My team had emphatically told these volunteers to pay close attention to each participant and to let us know if any were having difficulties.

One woman opted not to participate in the sweat lodge after listening to my description and cautionary warnings. That was completely acceptable by me and the entire group of participants. She left the site and went back to her room.

We had as much first-aid as we thought would be needed and more. One of the volunteers was a nurse, and one of the participants was a medical doctor. I had paid to have one of my team members become certified in CPR, which I believed to be only proactive and precautionary, because we had done this activity many years before and had never needed this. It seemed we were all good to go.

I was leading the experience inside the lodge. Between the registered participants, my team, and my team of volunteers, we had approximately fifty-six people in the lodge.

I opened the experience with a brief presentation, including instructions to exit the structure clockwise only at the end of each round when the door flap was opened if they felt they needed to leave. This was the second time I covered this. I covered it once prior in the Crystal Hall meeting room. I wanted to make sure they fully understood and had ample time to ask any clarifying questions.

Part of the group experience is verbalizing and calling out your intentions and prayers. During the early rounds of the ceremony I sing and pray in a mix of languages and traditions—Hebrew, Native American, and Latin. I call out for commitment from the participants and have them strongly verbalize those commitments. Traditionally we start in the east, the direction of the rising sun. In many traditions, each direction has similar symbols and representations.

The group shouts encouragement and congratulations to those who call out what they have let go or what they have committed to change.

Three participants left the lodge either during or immediately after the first round, unable to endure the intensity of the heat. Some of these returned in later rounds, some did not.

Some people made it through five or six rounds then exited. When people left, I would call to them during the round breaks encouraging them to come back in. Encouraging them to bring out the best within them. Some came back. Some didn't.

After the fourth or fifth round several people began to fully experience the drain on their body from the heat. Including me. Many had moved off the benches outside and were lying on the ground with their cheeks in the dirt, which offered some cooling relief. I had instructed them that the lower to the ground they got the cooler it would be.

Liz Neumanwas one of our Dream Team members—people who initially came through Spiritual Warrior as participants and were allowed to come back and help facilitate the event without paying the registration fee.

Liz told me prior to the lodge, "James, I just need you to know that I've felt lately that I really want to take a stronger leadership role in this work, and I need to step it up. I'm ready to do whatever I need to do to make that happen." Little did either of us know what that would mean.

During the lodge experience, Liz was posted on the northern side of the lodge to the left of where I was located, in the west. She chatted with some of the women she was sitting next to, periodically tapping them on the arm or the leg. They devised this system to let each other know they were okay.

When the person felt the tapping, they should respond with a similar rhythm of tapping to indicate that they were still there and pushing forward.

It was pitch dark inside the lodge.

During one of the later rounds I heard someone say, "James, I'm concerned about Liz."

I responded, "She's done this before. She knows what she's doing."

---

*I truly believed this to be true. To this day
I'm shocked and saddened at how wrong I was.*

---

The ceremony lasted for eight to twelve rounds—memory is unclear, as I wasn't really counting them. I was too immersed in the moment of the experience. Yet I do know it was approximately two hours. Several people passed out during the later rounds and were dragged out of the lodge by volunteers and other participants.

While passing out is intense, I'd seen it before. I was not insensitive to this. People pass out when running marathons and other physically grueling events as well. Even during panic attacks fainting often occurs. My experience was that once they were exposed to fresh air and water, their bodies would normalize. We had a trained team outside to assist in whatever was needed.

I knew that people were struggling, but struggle is part of the experience. Struggle is part of the experiential learning and the metaphor, for struggling is a part of life.

When the lodge experience was over, I was the first to exit, being next to the tent flap doorway. Little did I know as I slipped into the cool night air that in less than fifteen minutes life as I once knew it would end forever.

One of the team members hosed me down. Raising my arms into the sky as the cold water drenched my body, I felt victorious. Given my past experience, I assumed the others would feel elated and victorious upon their exit as well.

They did feel victorious. At least up to the point that we all realized something was terribly wrong.

As I sat in a folding chair cooling down, breathing and hydrating, I was mere minutes away from the life-death-rebirth metaphor becoming much more than a metaphor. Way more.

It became absolutely literal.

## CHAPTER 5

# DECISIONS IN CHAOS

When we came out of the lodge, it was near dusk. I was utterly drained and exhausted. The heat had taken a heavy toll on me.

I spotted an empty chair, grabbed a bottle of water, and made my way through the participants to sit down. As I gazed up at the clear twilight sky, grateful to have completed this ordeal for another year, one of the volunteers sprayed me with water while I rehydrated and caught my breath.

The scene appeared to me to be like the conclusion of any other sweat lodge we had conducted in prior years. Many were coming out elated. Thrilled that they had overcome and conquered this obstacle.

One woman in particular who had struggled with her own internal dialogue, demons, and abilities for years came out and thrust her arms into a victory pose. She was absolutely beaming. That made me feel great.

*Helping my clients get past their own limitations*
*and step into their own greatness is why I do what I do.*

Several people were lying on tarps, fatigued. I could see a few were struggling, but, based on past experience, I was certain everything would normalize in a few minutes.

Suddenly someone came running around from the back of the lodge and said, "There are two people down in the back of the lodge. Can we pull them out the back?"

I answered, "Yes, of course, if that's what needs to be done."

It still didn't register. My head was light and unclear from the experience. *Stay calm, James. Others heard this and they're looking to you as the leader for your reaction. Don't panic. Clear your head. What does this mean?*

As more participants came out of the lodge and their bodies reacted, the scene became chaotic. People were throwing up, moaning, and asking for help. Some were shaking and unable to walk.

I called out, "Where's the nurse?" Still doing my best to stay calm and centered.

Slowly, it dawned on me that more people than usual were in distress. Several were unconscious, foaming at the mouth, and not responding to efforts by team members to revive them.

I had *never* in all my years previously seen *anyone* foam at the mouth. *This is crazy. What's going on?*

A big commotion erupted on the back side of the lodge. I walked around to the back and saw Kirby Brown and James Shore lying on the ground. Their color was wrong. Very wrong. They were bluish and their lips were pale.

Someone said, "They're not breathing."

These words echoed in my mind and hung like a heavy anchor in the air.

## Liz Newman, Kirby Brown, and James Shore

I had built a very strong connection with both Kirby and James during the entire week of the event. Now they were lying on the ground in front of me—and they were not reviving.

James and Kirby had been sitting together in the lodge. At some point near the middle of the ceremony, Kirby started rocking her body back and forth and repeating her verbal affirmations loud enough that everyone could hear her.

"We can do it. We can do it. We can do it." It was so loud and constant that for many it became annoying.

Several people asked her to stop because she was disturbing their private experience. Kirby persisted nonetheless. One of the participants became agitated and asked her to stop several times, with an intensity that escalated from a request to a demand, but Kirby still continued.

James never left the lodge during any of the early rounds. Kirby never left the lodge during any of the round breaks. As other participants left the ceremony, space in the lodge freed up and both James and Kirby laid down in the back on the ground.

During one of the later rounds James Shore became aware that a young woman seated near him was not doing well. At the next break, he asked someone to help him carry her out. After exiting and getting the young woman settled outside, James returned of his own choice and resumed his position next to Kirby. Her breathing had become heavy and according to some reports she was making gurgling, snorting sounds.

I was unfortunately unaware of this. All I heard was, "We can do it. We can do it. We can do it."

Again, several participants asked her to "shut up," but she continued. James was lying next to her and was talking to her almost constantly, offering support and telling her she could make it. He also replied to others when asked if Kirby needed help, saying that he "had her taken care of."

A woman sitting near Kirby called out several times that Kirby needed to be taken out because she was delirious. James Shore responded, "She's fine. I've got this covered." The woman who expressed concern told James they should roll her over on her stomach to help her breathing. Kirby reportedly was no longer responding rationally.

"We can do it. We can do it. We can do it."

James sat up and tried to reposition Kirby, but he could not shift her weight by himself. The woman used her legs and pushed Kirby up just enough so James could roll her over. The gurgling breathing did not stop. James constantly reassured her. He told Kirby she was okay. Several people stated, "Kirby needs help," and James Shore responded, "No, she's okay, I've got this."

In one of the final rounds there was a flash of light inside the lodge when someone raised the blankets that formed the side opposite me. Given the location of the light, it may have been James trying to give Kirby some air. The record does show that one participant lifted up the flap and rolled out of the lodge over near James and Kirby. He'd had enough and this was his quickest exit.

For some strange reason, in my own clouded thinking, I thought someone had brought a flashlight into the lodge.

"No, no, you can't do that. That is dishonorable. This is a sacred space," I yelled in their direction, having no idea what was unfolding across the 25-foot span of the lodge. The light was immediately extinguished.

Now standing outside the backside of the lodge, looking at James and Kirby with their blueish skin and pale lips, and observing the scene around me, I became frantic. I couldn't fathom what was going on. People were performing CPR on several individuals, including James and Kirby. I'm not trained in CPR, but I had team members who were. My team and I had made sure of that in advance.

This is a key distinction for a leader to understand. Sometimes you must step back and trust the experts to do their job. Your job is to make sure they do it. In this case, the experts were my own team members. I had entrusted them with their respective jobs, so it was time for me to step back, remove all obstacles, make decisions, and let them perform the job they were hired and trained to do.

I remained a few steps back because I didn't want to get in the way. Dr. Jeanne Armstrong was standing to my left, and I asked, "Jeanne, is there any way we can get them back?"

She said, "James, don't worry. I've seen people like this before, and when the EMTs get here they probably can be revived." That gave me a degree of hope. I needed hope.

"What else do we need to do?" I asked.

She replied, "If there's a defibrillator on property, we need that." I took off to find the owners and see if they had a defibrillator. Never before had we thought it necessary to have such a device. In retrospect I should have.

## Breathe. Relax. Prioritize. Act.

Leaders often have to make decisions in the midst of total chaos. And if ever I needed to make decisions as a leader in the midst of total chaos, that time was now. Leaders must will their chaotic lower self to breathe, relax, prioritize, then act.

Depending on the situation, this entire process often happens in the blink of an eye. It has to. There's no time for over-thinking, no time for analyzing. There's only time for acting. No matter how limited the information on hand may be.

## Calmness Through Chaos

Finally, I heard sirens and knew that medical help was on the way. The ambulances and fire trucks all arrived in a swarm, adding to the sense of chaos. Several people were placed on gurneys and put onto oxygen machines. IVs were inserted and EMTs were running back and forth with equipment. Others radioed for additional assistance, including helicopters to airlift the most urgent cases to the hospital in Sedona.

I was doing my best to keep people calm and out of the way.

Those who appeared to be in good shape, I encouraged to return to their cabins. I told them we would all meet in the dining hall later after they cleaned up. I had to behave with certainty and congruity.

In this moment of chaos, I still believed we would all circle back and debrief. Some people who were not doing so well were screaming, reacting from the fear of ambulances, helicopters, and EMTs. I tried to calm them down.

The EMTs quickly had the situation under control. My director of technology came up to me and said, "James, you need to go back to your room and get cleaned up. We've got to gather these people together to debrief and finish the event."

I looked deeply in his eyes; we were both in shock and denial to some degree. To his leadership credit, he was maintaining his composure well. Particularly for his limited years of life and business experience.

Typically, after the sweat lodge ceremony everyone came back into the Crystal Hall for a grand finale celebration. In my mind, I was thinking: *We've got to get people fed. I've got to figure out how to deal with this because people are upset.* I was stepping into my role as the event leader, not yet fully realizing the gravity of what was happening. I followed his suggestion and went back to my room to regroup.

Soon after I left the sweat lodge area, the place was flooded with police. They asked the team members who was in charge. The police were told that I was in charge and that I was in my room.

This was one of the first logs to stoke the bonfire of bad press to follow.

A great deal was made of the fact that I was "in my room" during the trial and in the media that reported the story. I understand that it looks bad out of context, but in context, the EMTs were there. They were trained and equipped to handle those in need of medical help. James and Kirby had already been flown out via helicopter. The rest of the clients had been sent back to their rooms to clean up and get themselves together physically and mentally. Some of the clients and participants not in need of medical help were in various degrees of shock or hysteria. I was better equipped to deal with them than anyone. I needed to get my head together so I could help them do the same.

---

### You cannot give what you don't have.

---

How was I going to support the participants who still remained at the ranch? I am reminded of the footage of President Bush in front of the children after being told about the Twin Towers toppling. If he had freaked out and gone into visible chaos, it would have just created more of the same.

I was still in shock. What the hell had just happened? This was not the norm. Not even close. Something was not right. I needed to collect my thoughts and sift through the noise in my mind so I could do just that. I needed to act, not react.

I was still desperately hanging on to the statement from Dr. Jeanne Armstrong that James and Kirby could be revived, and that she'd seen this situation before. I was hanging on with all hope. *After all, she's an MD*, I continually told myself.

At this point, I had no idea Liz Neumanwas also in trouble.

## And So It Begins

As I was in the shower, doing my best to clear my head, I heard someone banging on the door. They kept banging.

"I am in the shower, and I'll be with you in a minute," I yelled from the bathroom.

"It's Officer _____, and I need to speak with you immediately."

"Give me just a minute, Officer," I said, realizing that all plans for devising a perfect strategy were over.

The press stated that they found me eating a sandwich. That's how they framed it, as if I were totally unconcerned. While this might be sensational, it's far from the truth. My meal was sitting on the table next to the door because the kitchen staff had brought it to my room on a pre-arranged schedule.

I was still thinking all participants were going to meet in the Crystal Hall. I had to deal with upset participants, clients, friends, and team members, and find a way to get them to a state of equilibrium. I hadn't even touched my dinner. Nor did I have any appetite whatsoever.

I opened the door wrapped in a bath towel.

"Are you James Ray?"

"Yes, I am."

"I need to see you down at the sweat lodge immediately."

I knew by the tone of his voice that this was big trouble.

I threw on a quick pair of shorts and flip-flops and walked with wet hair following the officer back to the sweat lodge area. The cold night air sent chills up my spine and throughout my entire body.

The first question the detective asked was, "Who's in charge of putting this lodge together?"

I told him that Ted Mercer and the owner of the ranch put the lodge together. Angel Valley Ranch supplied all the materials, all the construction, all the storage—everything belonged to Angel Valley Ranch.

None of my team members ever touched *anything* during the construction of the lodge. Not a stick, stone, blanket, or tarp. I answered his question literally.

The press spun that statement into an indication I didn't want to take responsibility for being in charge of the lodge. That was not what I meant at all. I was answering the exact question he asked. My team had not put the lodge together, and that was the truth.

"Were you in there?"

I said, "Yes, I ran the experience."

Then the detective said, "I hope you know we're investigating this as a homicide." Everything went silent. I glanced over at the lodge; they had already roped off the area with yellow crime scene tape.

*A homicide?* My head started spinning, and I said, "I've got to call my lawyer."

I didn't have a criminal lawyer. Why would I? I worked with Greenburg & Glusker at the time. A law firm who drew my contracts and transactional work. I immediately called Hillary, the lawyer with whom I had a good working relationship. It was late. I had her personal cellphone number because we did a lot of business with the firm, and she answered.

I said, "Hillary, I'm in trouble." I told her what the detective said and asked her what I should do. She contacted a criminal lawyer she knew and had gone to school with. Her friend Steve called me back immediately.

Steve said, "Look, you must do exactly what I tell you to do. You might go to jail tonight. If you do, we'll get you out as soon as we can."

I thought, *Jail? Are you kidding me?* My head was spinning fast, and I thought I just might throw up.

Steve said, "Don't answer any more questions. Under no circumstances. No matter what they ask you, do not answer the questions." He had a tone of authority and experience in his voice.

When my attorney told me, "Don't answer another question," I followed orders. I didn't answer any more questions. The vision of James and Kirby lying on the ground blue with pale lips played over and over across the screen of my mind. It was punctuated with the words "homicide" and "jail." It echoed incessantly in my mind like the music from a bad horror movie.

It was surreal. Beyond shock.

To not answer questions didn't sit very well with the detectives. I said, "I've been instructed by my legal counsel not to answer any more questions."

That was later interpreted in the media and the trial as: James Arthur Ray was not cooperative with authorities. I get it. But remember, when you're read your rights, it's stated that "anything you say can and will be used against you in a court of law." It also states, "You have the right to remain silent." I claimed this right. Just as instructed.

Homicide is serious. I still couldn't get my mind around it. Were they serious?! There had to be some mistake. Jail was terrifying. Talking to a criminal lawyer was surreal.

## Protecting My Team

About 6 p.m., they put me in the back of a patrol car. I'd never been here before. Never expected I would be. I sat on the hard plastic seat, my knees up to my chin and jammed against the front seat because there wasn't room for my legs. These cars are not built for comfort. Far from it. They're built for containment.

The officer closed the door and left me in the patrol car for what seemed an eternity. At one point, I tried to open the door and found that it doesn't open from the inside. These cars are not designed for comfort *or* willful exit.

I looked over at one point and saw that two of my other team members were also in patrol cars. One of them was Josh, my Director of Technology. Josh was in his early thirties and looked as scared as I felt. I had no idea why they detained Josh and others until later, nor did I realize at the time the significance it would play in the outcome.

Finally, the owner of Angel Valley Ranch walked by, and I rapped on the window. I gestured to have him open the door and he did. I stuck my legs out, stood up, and actually got out of the car to let the blood circulate because I was so cramped and still incredibly dehydrated, tired, and hungry.

An officer came over, and I thought he was going to tell me to get back in, but he didn't. I left the door open from that point on and stretched my legs sideways out the door. As the evening progressed, the temperature dropped. It was freezing cold, and I only had on a t-shirt, shorts, and flip-flops. They kept me in the patrol car for eight hours, until 2 a.m.

Much of this time I was on the phone off and on with the new attorney. Steve said, "What are they telling you?"

"They're not telling me anything, and I'm frantic."

"Let me talk to the officer."

The officer came by, and I said, "My attorney would like to speak with you. Will you talk with him?" They talked briefly. The officer gave the phone back to me.

Steve told me, "It doesn't look like they're going to arrest you tonight. They don't have enough evidence." This was a huge relief.

He also told me that it was far from over, and there was a definite possibility they could come after my team as well. After all, the event was a company event and we were all employees of the company. I hadn't even considered until that point that there could be implications on my team as well. I was still perplexed as to why there were even implications on me.

This was much worse and much bigger than I thought. Now my entire team could be at risk?

No matter how many times my attorney said the words "homicide," "arrest," and "jail," it just wasn't registering with me. I couldn't wrap my mind around it. Now he was saying the same thing about my team? None of it made sense.

Wasn't this obviously an accident? Would I, as the leader of my business and team, willfully hurt any of our clients?

In the meantime, my personal assistant, Taylor, came over and said, "James, they've seized your room. There's an officer sitting in your room, and he's going through your bags."

They took my vitamin supplements and prescription medications, threw them on the bed, and took pictures of them all. For what purpose, I'll never know.

These pictures ended up posted all over the internet, evidence of what, I'm not sure. I felt incredibly violated. I'm an extremely private person, and not used to parading my personal life around the world. Yes, I'm a public figure, but I find that the more public my business life becomes the more sacred my private life is for me.

I asked Taylor to get my computer bag and wallet out of my room if possible. She was able to get the computer bag and wallet, but not the computer because they had seized it. They also took my personal journal. My journals have always been sacrosanct to me. This was unbelievable. I kept thinking this nightmare would break any moment and I would wake up. But it just kept coming.

When they released me, it was now past 2 a.m. There was an officer posted in my room, and all my bags had been seized.

My first thought was that I had to get to Crystal Hall and meet with my team. Yet when I arrived everyone was gone. Some had gone to sleep, others left the property. I saw a light on at the owners' home on the hill. I walked up and found what remained of my team. Like me, they were all exhausted and in complete shock.

They were trying to figure out their next best move. With their leader detained, they kicked into gear. Like diligent soldiers they were doing their best to get their minds around it and decide what to do next. They were stepping up as they always did.

---

*True leaders don't create followers. They create more leaders.*

---

While I was in custody, my team had been hard at it. I don't believe any of us understood even a fraction of what was to come. In fact, I'm certain of it.

Even though we didn't know it, our days as a team and a company were numbered, and the clock was ticking rapidly. Like a time-bomb.

I met with them and received a status update. I called my new criminal defense attorney, Steve, once again, "They're not going to arrest me tonight and yet my room is seized."

"James, get out of there. We need to meet in my office first thing tomorrow morning."

That wasn't what I wanted to do. Every fiber of my being wanted to go to the hospital and be with James, Kirby, and Liz. Steve said no way. The hospital was crawling with press, police officers, and family members. Two of those groups wanted nothing more than to talk to me. To possibly either get me to say something incriminating or at least something that could be spun into sensational press coverage.

The other parties, the families, did not want to see me, according to Steve. Later interaction would prove Steve absolutely correct. "James, this is serious business for you and your team," Steve said. "If you go to the hospital and speak to anyone, you could be in grave danger of implicating yourself and your team."

His words rang in my ears like a large gong. Implicate my team.

What to do? Leaders must make decisions.

---

### *Breathe. Relax. Prioritize. Act.*

---

*If I leave the property, it may be spun negatively in the press. It most probably will be. It may also be perceived by the families and my clients that I don't care. That I'm just looking out for myself. I'll be misunderstood at best and possibly attacked. I'll take massive vitriol for that decision on multiple levels.*

*Yet if I follow my emotions and go to the hospital, I may say something off-the-cuff and put my team in danger.*

Homicide is a serious issue.

Both options were less than ideal.

## A Decision to Make

I decided to listen to Steve's voice of experience. It was part of my responsibility as a leader. I had to put my emotions aside and trust the advice of my attorney. Believe me, I argued with him. I had to get to the hospital—but he wasn't backing down.

Imagine you're climbing Mount Everest with a very experienced guide. He's summited Everest more times than you can count. You've hired him and you're paying him well for his experience and expertise.

At one point you *really* want to take this interesting trail that goes in a different direction than he suggests. He admonishes you firmly and tells you it's dangerous, and he tells you exactly why. He tells you it's not only dangerous for you, but it may also endanger the entire party.

Do you ignore the voice of experience?

To do what you "want" to do in spite of great counsel would be imprudent, irresponsible, and maybe even stupid.

I listened to Steve.

From a leadership perspective, I made the decision to leave Angel Valley. Sometimes in a leadership role you have to consider more than your own personal desires. You have to think about all implications. Not just your own. You have to make the best decision with the information you have, and that's exactly what I faced. You have to subjugate emotion to logic.

All I wanted to do at that point was go to the hospital and be with Liz, my clients, the families, and others. Or, at the very least, just be there to make sure my greatest fears weren't going to be realized. I wanted to check on all my clients. I wanted to do whatever I could to ease their angst and pain. That was the *entire* thrust of the week.

Yet I had to trust the advice of my lawyer, as much as I wanted not to.

As it turned out, my attorney was exactly right. My team was at risk of being indicted as employees of the company. In the end, the team members were offered immunity by the DA in exchange for their testimony. The DA was hopeful they would tell them something that would incriminate me. I told them just to tell the truth. The truth is the only thing that needs no defense.

Had I followed my own personal preference and gone to the hospital that night, things could have turned out very differently.

## Media Frenzy

I called my assistant Amy, saying, "You've got to find me a flight and get me out of here as soon as possible."

"What's wrong?" she asked.

"I can't tell you right now, Amy, but it's bad."

She sent a car for me but couldn't get a flight until the crack of dawn the next morning. She booked a hotel room for the night, but I didn't sleep a wink. My mind was racing at 1,000 mph.

At dawn I turned on the television, and the story was all over the news.

They had photos of the sweat lodge and video of the scene with all the flashing lights from the emergency vehicles and helicopters. The newscaster said, "James Arthur Ray has fled the scene."

The story was already being distorted in the press, and I was quickly on the way from being media star, *New York Times* bestselling author, and Inc. 500 inductee to "sweat lodge guru." My entire life got wiped away and was now defined by a fateful two hours and a tragic accident.

## Absolute Responsibility

When I arrived at the airport the next morning, I was a fugitive. I did not get my bags from the police, so I only had the clothes on my back. At some point, my PA Taylor had retrieved some long pants and sneakers for me from my seized room. She also got my wallet, because I wouldn't have been able to board the plane without ID.

I sat in the airport, with a ball cap pulled way down over my eyes. The TVs were blaring from every gate in the airport hyping the sweat lodge story. I was over in the corner with my head down. Everywhere I went I heard, "James Arthur Ray has fled the scene."

I can't even begin to tell you how that felt. It was extremely uncomfortable to be in my own skin. This was the antithesis of everything I had built my life upon. Little did I know things were about to get much worse, with so much gone in the blink of an eye.

I now knew James and Kirby were gone, and Liz was in the hospital on life support. I had a criminal lawyer, and I was a "fugitive." They were potentially coming at me with a homicide charge. My team might also be indicted. I shrank into the corner of the airport, praying not to be seen. *How can any of this be happening?*

Here we are again, back to Absolute Responsibility. All I could think was, *What a mess I've made here.* I was trying to do something good, now the implications were vast. From James, Liz, and Kirby, their families, my clients and participants, to my team, I suddenly felt a tremendous albatross of responsibility and consequence weighing on me.

I was the guy who built his entire life around helping people make the best of difficult situations. Now here I sat giving myself pep talks, repeatedly telling myself that everything was going to be okay. But I frankly didn't believe it.

When I look back on it now, I have an immense understanding for leaders in the military. You can only try to imagine how it must feel for a military leader to lose some or all of his soldiers. On his watch.

The main difference was he leads his soldiers into battle knowing the real possibility that they all might not return. Never in my wildest dreams could I have imagined that I would be faced with the same. Except suddenly here I was.

Like a military leader, I was leading people into a battle with their own personal demons. Pushing and hoping for them to come out of it victorious.

Like you, I'd heard and read the stories of military leaders who lose troops. Up until that point I couldn't have imagined what that feels like. To lose people you had grown to know and care for. People for whom you only wanted the best, people you wanted to see succeed. People who trusted you and followed your direction.

Now I knew.

I thought of their families. The pain and agony they must be feeling. And, understandably, the anger. While I had entered into that weekend with the very best of intentions—a desire to help and transform lives—suddenly my intentions were worthless.

Lives were changed, but not in the way that I had hoped. Two lives were ended. A third hung in the balances.

I flew to LA and immediately went to meet my attorney Steve for the first time.

Steve met me at his office elevators. He shook my hand and introduced himself. "How are you doing?"

The voice of deep denial and shock answered, "You know, I'm doing pretty well." Mr. Growth, Inspiration, and Strategy was now Mr. Bullshit. I wasn't doing well at all.

I know why he was surprised by my response. He'd been here many times before. He knew a lot more about the magnitude of the situation than I ever could. I still hadn't fully grasped the reality of what was unraveling around me. I was the master of reframe. I was doing everything I could possibly do to put a positive spin on something that could never be spun.

Yet how desperately I needed to, for my own mental survival.

Over time, my attorneys helped me pull away the layers until we got to the core of pain and anguish.

But this was just the beginning of a very long and painful journey. Just the tip of the iceberg.

## CHAPTER 6

# BESIEGED

My whole life had been about helping people find their greatness and break through their own self-limitations. This was the absolute antitheses of everything I had centered my life around. It was ineffable. Beyond words to describe.

But now my life was more in shambles than ever before. More in shambles than anyone I'd ever worked with.

I needed to get my own life in order fast if I wanted to continue helping others do the same. This was a tall order. Yet you can't lead anything until you can effectively lead your own life. It seemed an impossible task in the moment, but I knew I must do it. I still had events to run. Clients had invested in them, purchased airline tickets and hotel rooms, and they were relying on me to deliver on that investment.

I had no time for the luxury of self-absorption. Every fiber of my being wanted to curl up in the fetal position and be left alone as the media hammered me from all sides. Yet I couldn't lose sight of the big picture because I still had a team to lead and a business to run. At least for the moment. Clients and team members counted on me to pull it together and do what they relied on me to do—I had to keep going and keep leading.

The very next week we were scheduled to do a major event called the World Wealth Summit, which was an annual event I conducted bringing together experts from many different fields. It had been booked for a solid year.

People had purchased tickets well in advance and were traveling from all over the globe to attend. We had been marketing the event heavily for months. There was an ongoing conversation between my PR agent, the lawyer, and me, where we asked, "Should we cancel? Or should we go ahead?"

I didn't feel right canceling the event because people had purchased non-refundable airline tickets. My friends and colleagues had blocked off their schedules and planned their travel as well.

We needed to honor our commitments.

Even though in my current state of mind it was the last thing in the world I wanted to do, we decided to go ahead with the World Wealth Summit the very next weekend. I was miserable. On the outside I did my best to keep it together, but inside I was an emotional basket case.

Normally, when you drop me onstage, I light up. But in this situation, I didn't even want to be there. James and Kirby were dead. Liz Neuman was still in the hospital in intensive care, and her very life hung in the balances. As much as we all hoped and prayed she would pass a few days later in the ICU.

We did our best, at the Summit, to pay homage to these friends. We set up a memorial in the room with two big white pillars, we had a moment of silence, and said a prayer for them. I prayed deeply and continuously for my friend Liz.

The entire weekend I struggled with thoughts of James and Kirby, and I worried for Liz. I had a responsibility to my team and to the attendees, and I wrestled to reconcile that with the deep sadness and overwhelming sense of responsibility I felt for those I had lost. I also had responsibility for Liz, who I was about to potentially lose.

The itinerary indicated I had two hours of time in front of the audience before I was scheduled to introduce any of the guests. Normally, this is not a big deal for me. I was known for having to figure out a way to fit all that I wanted to share into a finite timeframe.

That day I presented for about fifty minutes of the two hours, then sent everyone on break. Fifty minutes felt like fifty days. It was everything I could do to keep it together. My team came up and said, "James, what are we doing?"

"I don't know, I can't do any more," I said. But I pushed through it. I reached deep into my beliefs and teachings to find the mental fortitude and grit I so desperately needed to continue. I owed it to the attendees, and I owed it to the memory of James and Kirby and the hope and prayer for Liz.

How could I back away now from the very thing I tried to instill in everyone who attended Spiritual Warrior? How could I not hold tight to my own teachings about reaching above and beyond obstacles to achieve harmony in life? To find the good, God, and gift amid the struggle and pain? How could I not push through my own anguish to find strength like I had encouraged my clients to do?

My last free intro event was scheduled for the following week in Toronto. Like the Summit, it had been on the calendar for a long time. Once again, we deliberated whether to cancel. My lawyer said, "I think you need to conduct it." My PR guy said, "Yeah, let's go ahead."

So I flew to Toronto. Never before had the old saying "the show must go on" felt as painful to me as it did right then.

My good friend and early coach Bob Proctor (who lives in Toronto) came to my hotel room prior to the event. He said, "James, you can't go out there. I had to wade through the press to get in the building. They've got trucks, vans, cameras, and towers. They're going to crucify you."

"But I have a responsibility to all these people," I said.

He was adamant. "You didn't see what I saw out there. It's a sea of cameras out there. *Good Morning America* is here. *The Today Show* is here. They're going to eat you alive."

---

### Breath. Relax. Prioritize. Act.

---

I called Mark, my PR agent, and said, "Here's the situation." I laid it out for him.

He said, "Well, James, if you don't perform, they're going to crucify you for not performing."

I said, "Yeah, I've got an absolute no-win here, Mark."

After much deliberation, we decided to pull the plug. My event coordinator made an announcement outside the room—we always kept the doors closed until the event started. She apologized and told the crowd we were not going to be able to hold the event. People were upset. Even though it had been a free event, there was still a lot of grumbling and disappointment. The press was particularly disgruntled because they had flown in from all over the country as well as from the US. The lobby was overflowing with press and camera crews.

Bob said, "Man, let's get out of here and get something to eat." Security escorted us through the back of the house because we knew the minute the press saw me they would stick a microphone in my face. We slid out the back door, jumped in Bob's car, and bolted.

## Media Frenzy, Round Two

**Anderson Cooper** covered the story on CNN. He had a picture of me flashing forward and back—expanding and contracting. Cooper said, "I want you to know who this guy is. He's still at large, he's still out there, and you need to know what he looks like."

It made no sense to me at all. What was I going to do? Whip out a sweat lodge and stuff people into it?

**Larry King** called my personal cell phone. I didn't answer, and he left a message saying, "James, I'll give you a fair shot. Just come on the show." I believed Larry, but I was in no space mentally and emotionally to even speak to him, much less be interviewed. I never returned his call.

**Matt Lauer** wanted to interview me on *The Today Show*. They offered me a series of five full slots on five different days. One per day for an entire week. They offered to fly me in and pay all expenses for an entire week. We turned it down.

All of the sudden, I became "The Sweat Lodge Guru" and nothing more. Nobody was saying anything about any goodness, any contribution, or any value I had provided to the world. I just couldn't comprehend it. Only weeks before, these same media personalities wanted me to appear on their shows and talk about "Harmonic Wealth" and living a productive and fulfilling life. I was the golden boy. Now, suddenly, I was a fugitive from justice. And a murderer. And I was still "at large and dangerous."

Prior to the accident I had sent out a tweet from Spiritual Warrior, something to the effect of, "The Spiritual Warrior has conquered death and therefore he has no enemies in this life or the next." This comes straight out of the Toltec shamanic teachings.

We discussed some of these concepts during the Spiritual Warrior event. Even the apostle Paul of the Christian tradition stated, "I die daily." Obviously, this death was a spiritual-mental-emotional death, not literal. It didn't matter. The press had a field day. It was a complete tee-up for sensationalism.

My PR agent at the time convinced me that we should take the tweet down. This was a huge mistake. When you take something down, it doesn't disappear in the internet world. The press of course ran with that one—"James is trying to cover his tracks." They were depicting me as a cult leader. "He was obsessed with death, and now he's trying to cover his tracks by deleting his tweets."

Some of my past students issued statements to the press. "James Arthur Ray is arrogant. He's all about the money. You can't even talk to him."

I couldn't fathom how people who just a month prior had been telling me I had transformed their life could change their tune so quickly. People were saying all kinds of crazy things to the press. My heart was broken, and I was melting down.

## Shutting Down the Company

It was apparent that the State of Arizona was going for blood. They were coming after me with guns blazing.

Seizing their fifteen minutes of fame, the sheriff and other elected officials in Prescott, Arizona, went on the air with *"We are tough on crime"* statements. *"We have zero tolerance."* They were playing to the grandstands. Big-time.

The Arizona police came to my offices in Carlsbad, California, in the dead of night, knocked the door open, and ransacked the office. Turning over desks, emptying draws on the floor, ripping two massive (and very expensive) servers out of the wall, and literally tossing them in the back of a pickup truck. They confiscated desktop computers and laptops. Multiple thousands of dollars of equipment—looking for what? A sweat lodge conspiracy?

I was dumbfounded. "Isn't this America?" I asked my attorney. "Can they do this?" Unfortunately, the answer was yes.

What the State of Arizona left of my business, the bad press finished off. Little by little the media was driving the business to carnage. Product sales had come to a screeching halt. Event registrations tanked. People once ecstatic to attend events were now asking for refunds on their ticket purchases in droves.

Someone hacked our membership website and hooked it up to a kiddie porn website. A member of the group Anonymous threatened to take my site down.

Our merchant account processing company asked for a $2 million retainer.

My banks dropped my company, and me personally, like a bad habit.

And more. A lot more.

Several of my colleagues from the TLC mastermind group I cofounded sent an email to my assistant and said, "James is no longer a member of the Transformational Leadership Council. His membership is revoked effective immediately. Please take our pictures off your website now."

Not even the courtesy of a phone call. Just an email to my assistant.

Just weeks earlier these same people had been my "friends." I hadn't even been indicted yet.

Guilty before even charged.

I had a new book that was due to be released from my publisher Hyperion in the spring of 2010. We started getting calls from people who had written testimonials for the book, saying, "You can't use my testimonial."

The tsunami just kept coming, and momentum was just beginning to build.

I realized what I had to do. Even though it broke my heart, we had to shut down the company. The company it took me twenty years to build. Twenty years of seven-day weeks, sixteen-hour days.

Addressing the allegations and the legal action was obviously going to take every last ounce of energy and attention I had, so I gathered the whole team together in November of 2009, right before Thanksgiving.

I remember calling my young, devoted team into the conference room. They knew things were going badly. The look in their hopeful eyes made it difficult for me to keep it together. They believed in me. They believed in the purpose and the vision. They too had made tremendous sacrifices of time, energy, and effort. They so obviously wanted some words of encouragement from their leader. I'm sure they had an inkling of what I was going to say.

"Guys," I began, "I can't begin to express how much I love and appreciate you."

My voice cracked and my eyes filled with tears. I struggled to hang on. "You've given so much of your heart and soul to our purpose and this work." Now tears were streaming from their eyes as well.

*Damn, I've got to find a way to finish this. I owe them that.*

"I think you all know this is tragic. I'm sure you have an idea of how bad all the implications are. I wish I had different news for you, but I'm going to have to devote all my energy and efforts toward this situation. We're going to need to close down for now."

I cared about these guys. They were like family to me. They worked hard on the road with me and stayed up until 2 a.m. computing numbers, coaching and supporting clients, and setting up and tearing down event rooms. They ran on next to no sleep with me.

They had worked in the trenches with people who were in anguish and helped them find their breakthroughs.

I was the engine that drove the machine. It demanded my all. The company's success and revenue stream was all on me. I was the messenger, the content creator, and the product all combined. Now the company's product was becoming severely tarnished.

These guys depended on me and trusted me. Their families depended on me. Now, not only was I letting them all go right before the holidays, but, because the company was in sad shape financially, they weren't going to get a big severance to help them make the transition. It broke my heart. Twenty years of hustle, love, energy, effort, and vision were gone. Completely gone.

---

*The only time we truly fail is when we lose all hope and give up.*

The metaphor of "dying to the old to birth the new" was unfolding daily in my own life. Like Apostle Paul, I felt like I was dying daily. Yet where was the birth? Nothing seemed new. There was no birth to be found. It was *all* just death. *How could it get any worse?*

It got worse.

## The Dream Home

In March 2009 I moved into my dream home on Mulholland Drive in Beverly Hills. Until that time, I had investment properties and commercial real estate, but I was leasing my personal residence. My financial advisor suggested I invest in a personal residence. Taking care of myself financially had always been a low priority. I always put everything into the business. I had a meager personal savings account until I hired my investment advisor, and he chastised me.

I'm a homebody, so I thought: *I'm going to put all my love, all my attention, and all my energy into this place, and it's going to be my fortress of solitude. When I come home, I want to come home to a place where everything is just like I want it, and I never have to leave until it's time to do my work and fulfill my purpose again.*

The house had not been well taken care of prior to my purchase. The previous owners had cut off the water supply to the backyard, and all the plants were completely dead. It was really in poor condition when I purchased it, but I had a vision.

When I was in town in 2009, usually only on weekends, my dream home to be was constantly under renovation and construction. There was so much work to be done.

In October, when I returned from Sedona, the house was still not finished. This time the homecoming felt dark and depressing. What once felt exciting and uplifting now fell flat. The work that had been completed while I was away didn't even matter to me. It had been my Sistine Chapel. Now I didn't care.

As I awakened to the situation I was facing, I realized that all my assets and income would be redirected toward my defense. This realization came to me little by little. As much as I loved the home, I had to halt the work and conserve my resources.

In November, I called the real estate agent and said, "Put the house on the market."

She said, "Are you nuts?"

My agent Dara and I had become close. She knew the love and care I was putting into my fortress of solitude.

I said, "I'm in a very bad situation. I feel it in my gut, Dara. It's bad. I need to put it on the market."

Because the house was so impeccably appointed, she felt like we could sell it furnished. This is common in Beverly Hills when homes are unique and professionally decorated.

I quickly started to cut back and made moves to consolidate money. I was spending so much money on legal fees that it was making my head spin. The massive retainer I sent to the lawyers was extinguished in the blink of an eye. Literally in a matter of weeks it was just gone. I stopped making payments on my rental properties as well as my investment properties. I put my commercial office space on the market.

In 2008-9, the real estate market tanked. Not a good time to be in financial straits with most of your money tied up in a defunct business and plummeting real estate. I owed $1.4 million on my office space. I brought the bank a short sale offer for $950,000 and change. This was a really good offer given the massive upheaval in the market.

My primary banker said, "We're not going to take that."

"Are you kidding me?" I said, "Look, it's really a great offer. I'm out of money."

During the bailout, the banks were being subsidized by the government, so the bank declined the offer. With government subsidies, they just didn't care. They didn't have to. The rub was that they were given trillions of dollars but no guidelines or parameters as to what they must do with the money. Unfortunately, they hoarded it versus investing it back into the economy. Really bad leadership call.

*Understanding human nature and setting parameters is paramount in leadership.*

The banker responded, "You don't have any money? I guess you won't have any worries when we come after you for the difference then will you?"

This was the same banker, who, just months before, was sitting in my office sucking up and telling me how I was one of their best clients, and that they were going to give me a million-dollar line of credit just on my signature.

I did business with several banks, so I went to a different one that I'd had a long-term relationship with. They told me, "Your accounts are closed."

I sat down with the president and said, "What's going on?"

"We don't want your business."

"Wait a second. Have I not been a great client?"

"That's not the issue."

"Have I not been with you for numerous years?"

"That's not the issue."

"Well, what the hell is the issue?"

"We just can't do business with you any longer."

They dropped me. They didn't have to tell me why. I knew why. The media monster had done its job well.

This was just the beginning of a long list of similar experiences. I had to scramble and find new banks. Any one of these things is an inconvenience by itself, but amid everything else I was juggling, it was catastrophic. I tried to close accounts. Because I was not paying mortgages, the lenders were coming at me for being in arrears.

I had cash in an account at a bank where I had a healthy business line of credit. Bad move. They swept the account. Several hundred thousand dollars. There one day, gone the next. I needed that money for my defense. The loss of that money hurt badly in a time when every dime was invested in fighting for my life and liberty.

I emptied all my bank accounts and put the money into cashier checks, which I kept in the safe in my house. By now it was no longer a "dream home," it was just a house. Funny how quickly a different perception creates an entirely different reality.

Then I got a call from the merchant account provider for my company: "We need a $2 million retainer."

"What?"

"We need a $2 million retainer because of all the negative publicity. We need to cover potential chargebacks."

"There is no way in hell I can afford to do that right now. Let me get this straight. There are no chargebacks of that magnitude, right?"

"Right."

"I can't pay that."

"Well, if you don't pay it, it will constitute a breach of contract, and we're coming after you."

*What the hell?*

Simultaneously, the families of James Shore and Kirby Brown filed civil suits against me. I hadn't purchased enough liability insurance to cover this type of catastrophic situation. Poor advice by my advisor. Yet it was my responsibility for listening to him.

---

**As a leader it's all your absolute responsibility.**

---

I made the best choice with the information I was given. Leaders often don't have time to second guess or analyze or research. Even when you know you're the one who will ultimately be standing in the crosshairs if things go sideways. At some point you have to trust your team and realize that *everything* is a risk.

Most days it felt like more than I could handle. Every single day brought another sucker-punch in the gut, a left hook, and a kick in the teeth. *Keep dodging and weaving, James. Get back up. Don't give up. Keep going.*

Talking to my Zen master mentor and friend one day, I said, "I can't take it anymore."

He said, "Yes, James, you *can* take it. In fact, ask for more."

More? I could barely handle what was unfolding around me let alone start piling on more.

*Where'd you get your bedside manner?* I thought. *From a butcher?*

His comment infuriated me. It was the last thing I wanted to hear. In retrospect, he was right. I could take more, and he knew what I didn't. Like it or not, more *was* coming.

---

*True leaders and mentors care enough*
*not to tell you what you want to hear.*
*Rather, they tell you what you need to hear.*

---

I now realize that adversity is our greatest ally. Nietzsche reminded us, "That which does not kill us makes us stronger."

Your struggles and scars become symbols of your strength.

I loved Nietzsche in college, yet being attracted to a concept is vastly different from real life experience. I felt like I was drinking water through a fire hose every single day and just doing my best not to drown.

My Beverly Hills home was in a gated neighborhood, and thank God, the security guards knew who I was and what I was dealing with. When process servers show up, security guards are required by law to let them in. The guards, however, liked me and felt for me. I had always been very kind and respectful to them, so they would let the process server through the gate and then quickly call me, saying, "Mr. Ray, we're sorry, but someone's coming to serve you. We're required to let them in."

Oh my God.

I would run around and turn the lights off in the house and stay out of view from the windows. It was self-preservation, a desperate move. The guards would see the furious servers returning from my home with their papers. They knew exactly what I was doing. Talk about demeaning. All pride and self-respect disappeared. I felt irresponsible, like a delinquent who didn't know what to do next.

Once I had been the image of success and achievement. Not anymore.

I just couldn't bring myself to allow the process server to serve me with legal papers at my own front door. Emotionally, I just couldn't take that on top of everything else.

I can't count how many times I had to do this. I stopped answering my phone because it was most often bill collectors. Most of my so-called friends had evaporated, never to be heard from again. How the collectors got my number, I'll never know because I *never* gave out my personal number, and it was unlisted and blocked. Then the press got my phone number. I stopped answering the phone altogether. I only responded to voice mail from people I wanted to speak to. Which wasn't many.

My home was right on Mulholland Drive with a large wall around it. Somehow, pictures of my backyard appeared on the internet, taken from over the fence. Where were the security guards? How were these people getting in?

Reporters are amazing at what they're able to weasel into. Maybe they got on one of those double-decker Hollywood tour buses and shot pictures over the wall. The tour buses stopped outside my neighborhood daily. I'll never know. Pictures of my entire backyard and pool were on the internet, and not real estate pictures either. These were pictures with my personal items and décor.

This and more became my life every single day, from October 2009 through February 2010. Five months felt like five years. Things were crumbling all around me.

It took everything I had to not succumb to the "why me?" mentality. So often when we find ourselves in seemingly impossible or traumatic situations that's our go-to question: *Why me?*

It wasn't until I lay staring at the four gray walls of my prison cell that I would learn the correct question we must ask: *Why NOT me?*

My life may have been crumbling to dust around me, but at least I had my life. James, Kirby, and Liz did not. It's all about perspective.

Remember? Life throws us curve balls. But curve balls can be hit. I needed to put my head down and start taking some practice swings. I needed to listen to the words of my Zen master friend—I could handle more. Knowing that helped get me through.

I was indicted in February 2010.

Day after day after day, through sheer willpower and discipline, I forced myself to get up in the morning. I didn't want to leave my house. There were days when I didn't think I could go on.

Every mode of escapism was appealing. I forced myself to go into my meditation room and try to quiet my mind, even though I was rarely successful. I knew that I *must* continue to function. I forced myself to try to think creatively and find assets I could liquidate. It was miserable. The guards kept calling. The process servers kept coming. The press kept calling. My so-called friends had vanished. The lawyers became my bosses.

I was powerless and drained and shattered. I was angry. I was so disenchanted and felt rejected and forsaken and betrayed. I remember being angry at God and angry at the world. It was incredibly painful. Beyond description.

## Legal Representation

I was not satisfied with my legal representation. I normally follow my intuitive nudges, most entrepreneurs do, and I just didn't feel right with Steve. I decided I needed a different lawyer but had no idea how to go about finding top quality criminal representation. Who does research on criminal lawyers? Whoever thinks they need to? Certainly not me.

I was driving back home from San Diego to LA, after the heart-wrenching meeting where I let my entire team go and shut down my company, when my phone rang. It was my friend Rhonda Byrne, one of the few people who stayed in contact and constantly checked in on me. I could count them on less than one hand.

She said, "How are you doing?"

"I'm not very good right now, Rhonda." And I told her what had happened.

She said, "Well, James, this is a bad situation. You need the best legal representation we can find. I want to introduce you to my attorney. He's an honorable man, and he's very talented. I need you to talk to him. His name is Brad Brian. I had a conversation with him about you last weekend. He's been following your case."

She continued, "Brad told me, just because something horrible has happened that was obviously an accident, it doesn't make it any better, or change it, by ruining another person's life."

My sentiments exactly.

"Will you talk to him?" she asked.

"Absolutely."

"Okay, I'll have him call you."

Before I got back home, my phone rang again, and it was Brad Brian. He said, "Look, James. I've been following this thing and there's absolutely no logic whatsoever in the fact that it's potentially being pursued as a criminal case."

He had a calm centeredness and a quiet confidence in his voice that was very appealing to me. He was a partner with Munger, Tolles, & Olson, generally referred to as MTO, which is considered one of the best law firms in the world.

He had a certainty about him: "James, if this thing goes the way it looks like it's going to go, it's simply wrong. There's no legal precedent for this. This should be a civil matter, at best."

Everything he stated gave me a great sense of calm. It gave me hope and a feeling I would be in capable hands. It was the life preserver I was trying to grab, but I was floundering and had yet to find it.

He said, "We need to meet," and I agreed. Boy did I ever agree.

I met Brad Brian and his partner, Luis Li, for lunch a couple days later in Beverly Hills. I couldn't talk about anything without bursting into tears. I was shattered. My once confident demeanor was completely gone. I was sitting in the restaurant blubbering and broken.

Luis and Brad were very patient and made me feel like the situation could become manageable. My gut told me *these are my guys.* I had already paid a healthy retainer to Steve. You learn very quickly that when retainers are paid to a lawyer, they're never meant to come back.

MTO was asking for an even larger retainer. My liquidity was not good. I had assets, but they were all tied up in real estate and the business. I had already almost exhausted my cash. What was I to do?

Assets with liabilities attached to them are not great assets when things go sideways. Just prior to Sedona, I had recently loaned $1.2 million of my own money to my company to make payroll and keep it afloat.

---

*Life as an entrepreneur is an endless dance between long-term opportunity and short-term need.*

---

Once again, as in so many situations in life and business, I had to make a leadership move. I had to make a decision between two less than perfect options. Conserve cash or make the big move, which felt right? Not knowing where the cash was going to come from made this especially difficult.

Years as a leader in my own business had taught me to make decisions based upon where you're going versus where you currently are. This was a key distinction that I taught my clients. It takes tremendous courage. It's often frightening as hell. But if you won't step up to this courageous move, you'll never have a prayer of getting where you have the potential to go.

---

*True leaders make decisions based upon where they're going versus where they are.*

---

I hired them anyway. It was a big bold move, and it was the right thing to do. I started the whole process over again with MTO.

We included several other attorneys on their team as well. The combined hourly rate of all these guys was staggering. They charged me for every email they read, as well as every phone call. When we'd get on the phone for a conference call, they'd have three lawyers on the phone, and all of them were billing for the call. There I was, with very limited capital left, my business worthless and gone, my real estate tanked and useless, and I had people suing me and bill collectors chasing me, six properties in some phase of foreclosure, $500,000 in legal retainers, and we were just getting started!

MTO decided to put together a white paper. They were going to assemble a comprehensive presentation of prior cases demonstrating the inappropriateness of the potential criminal charges against me.

Not only had there been numerous deaths in sweat lodges prior to mine, but none of them had *ever* been prosecuted as a crime. Not one.

The paper was very well researched, and it cost a fortune in billable hours. Over $300,000 to be exact! The strategy: "We'll present this to the DA, and she'll see the logic and drop the charges." It didn't work that way. Not even close.

This was not a case of either precedent or logic. It was a case of politics, power, and driving perceptions for election.

I got a phone call late one night from Luis Li. He said, "We turned in the white paper, James. The DA, Sheila Polk, has delegated the review of the document to one of her underlings. She won't even schedule a meeting with us to discuss it."

Her mind was made up.

He said, "James, this is not going well."

My heart sank and my stomach dropped. "What do you mean?"

He said, "I had a conversation with the prosecutor today, and I'm not getting a good feeling."

In addition, we had also retained a local Arizona attorney, Tom Kelly. Neither Brad nor Luis were licensed to practice in Arizona, so they needed an Arizona-licensed attorney to act as lead counsel who could file all the papers. I hired Tom Kelly so the MTO team could operate through his office.

Luis had a conversation with Tom Kelly earlier in the day and learned that the grand jury was convening the next day. They would make the decision regarding whether there was enough evidence against me to issue an indictment.

Little did we know at the time that the DA had called an illegal and unprecedented meeting with the coroners to agree upon the cause of death. This was to be later uncovered by the judge, and the DA attempted to suppress it. The coroners could not agree based on the evidence. The Arizona DA called all the coroners in, and Detective Ross Diskin created a PowerPoint presentation convincing them to agree upon heat as the cause.

This was not typical protocol.

The coroners are supposed to come to their own conclusions independently, not be encouraged with a dramatic PowerPoint presentation and solicited to concur.

Sheila Polk wanted this issue teed-up for the grand jury, and she got it. They would later be sanctioned and fined for this violation.

Luis continued on the phone call, "James, I need you to pack a small bag. We're going to Arizona tonight."

I said, "What?" I had no interest in returning to Arizona. My heart was racing. My mind spun.

He said, "The grand jury is meeting tomorrow, and I think this is going badly. The last thing in the world I want to happen is for the sheriff and a detective to show up at your home with cameras rolling, cuff you, parade you through the airport, or take you to the downtown LA county jail. James, I don't want you in the LA county jail." He emphasized this in no uncertain terms. "The LA county jail is a scary and dangerous place. Those guys have 'F*** You' tattooed on their eyelids."

I so didn't want to hear the word *jail*. I didn't want to even think about jail. Luis continued, "So we're going to Arizona, and if necessary, you're going to surrender. If they decide to indict you, you're going to surrender."

I was stupefied. The room was spinning. Suddenly, I felt like I would throw up.

He said, "How much money do you have left?" By this time, I had emptied out all that was left of my investment account and put it in the safe at my home, in cashier's checks.

Luis said, "I need you to give me all of your cashier's checks."

I was infuriated. I knew good and well that if I turned over this money, there would be nothing left, and I *knew* it was never coming back.

"James, we don't have time to argue this right now. I'll put it in an escrow account for you at Munger, Tolles, & Olson. That way, we will have it for your bail, if we need it."

Bail?

## CHAPTER 7

# INDICTED—INCARCERATED

On the long drive across the barren desert from Phoenix to Prescott, Luis Li and I talked about the Old Testament Book of Job. This was not an analogy I appreciated even though I felt as if I were living it. Sitting in my father's congregation in a small church in Tulsa, Oklahoma, all those years, I never dreamed I'd be able to relate to this story so fully.

Luis ensured me the entire drive that if I got indicted, my rights as an American citizen would really kick in. No more suppression of evidence. No more secret meetings with the coroners to coerce them into an agreement and conclusion. There were laws, and the game was going to change.

All this sounded good on some level, but the word *indicted* cut through my gut like a dull knife.

Luis is one of the most honorable men I know, and he truly believed everything he told me—even though his belief turned out to be severely in error.

We arrived in Prescott, Arizona, in the dead of night. The town was deserted at this late hour. We pulled into a small roadside inn for a sleepless night.

Prescott is a throwback to the Wild West. I was shocked the next morning to see guys wearing holstered guns on their hips both on the streets and in restaurants. Everywhere. Very disconcerting. *This is where my life is potentially going to be judged and tried?*

Luis and Tom kept assuring me that these people were gun-toting, severe right-wing Republicans. They were ranchers and "take care of yourself" type of people.

What they weren't accounting for was how the entire situation was going to be spun. I was the "cult leader" from Beverly Hills here to prey upon people's wills and wallets. The guy who charged people as much for one week as many here made in a year.

I was the poster boy for everything that anybody hated or had been disappointed about in the whole self-help industry, and it had been built up and pent up for decades.

The grand jury convened that morning at the Yavapai County Courthouse. We set up camp in Tom Kelly's office and waited while the grand jury deliberated. It was a grueling mental/emotional day to say the least.

The prosecutor, Sheila Polk, stood in front of the grand jury and presented her case. She put the lead investigator, Detective Ross Diskin, on the stand, and he shared the evidence he had assembled against me. My defense team was not allowed to be present during the grand jury proceedings. This was the largest potential case in Yavapai County history at the time and yet the very first case Diskin had ever been the lead detective on. He was out to show his stuff and make Ms. Polk proud.

The purpose of this hearing was to determine whether the prosecutor had enough evidence to find "probable cause" that I had committed the crime they wanted to charge me with.

Manslaughter. Intentional harm.

I'm a businessman, a serial entrepreneur. The very crux of my existence and my business is serving and helping people, not hurting them. This was the most ludicrous assertion I had ever heard, and it made no sense whatsoever. Lots of things didn't make sense. They didn't have to.

Logic and emotion are strange bedfellows, and in this case emotion was driving the bus. All logic had left the building. Actually, left the state.

I walked down Main Street in this small town to get some fresh air and grab some lunch in a small café. It felt as if every single eye was transfixed upon me. Drilling holes through me. Guys wearing guns on their hip was not something I was accustomed to, much less comfortable with. Particularly now.

I just knew in my gut it was going to go bad. I was the big-shot "criminal" in town. Little did I know that this greasy burger was the last meal I would have outside a cell for some time to come.

By the time I returned, Luis and Tom looked somber. They informed me that the grand jury decided there *was* sufficient evidence to indict me on manslaughter charges. I was shocked. Luis and Tom couldn't believe it either. This was not how it was supposed to play out. Manslaughter?

They explained that this was a positioning maneuver that gave the prosecution two shots to convict me. If I was acquitted on manslaughter, there was a "lesser included" charge of negligence. I was getting a quick and painful education on our legal system.

Later in the afternoon, three officers arrived at Tom's office to take me away. They were very respectful. One of them said, "I apologize for this, but we've got to cuff you."

I quickly slipped out of my jeans and put on a pair of sweatpants and a sweatshirt.

"I know these things are really uncomfortable," the officer said as he held out the cuffs. "I don't think you're going to run."

"No," I said, "you don't have to worry about that."

"Then I'll cuff you in front because it's a little more comfortable." They cuffed my hands in front of my body instead of behind. They treated me very respectfully. Almost apologetically.

The officer put me in the back of a police cruiser. I would later learn this was Detective Diskin, the man in charge of my investigation. I wouldn't learn until much later how little investigation was actually conducted. From the moment I was informed they were "investigating it as a homicide" on October 8, their sights were set and their minds made up.

As we drove, the officers said, "They're probably going to put you in protective custody. How are you feeling?" They were doing their best to be civilized. They knew I was scared, and this situation was shockingly surreal.

At one point, the driver's cell phone rang, and by this time it was getting dark. I could only hear his side of the conversation, but it was along the lines of, "Are you sure? We never take people in through the front door. Are we going to be able to get through the mob of press?"

The normal procedure was to take the person being arrested into custody through the back door into a gated area. But not me. It was show time!

My lawyers later told me that the DA and/or the sheriff, who had both been grandstanding about the case for weeks, were showing the public they had brought the dangerous fugitive into custody. This is what's known as a "perp walk." Parading the perpetrator prize in front of the world.

*"We landed the big gorilla."*

While on the phone, the officer expressed quite a bit of doubt as to whether bringing me through the front door was the right move. He ultimately acquiesced. He had to. It was his job, and he was getting orders from a higher rank. We pulled into the main parking lot of the Yavapai County Jail at Camp Verde, and the parade began.

I was the trophy arrest.

## County Jail

The press had packed the parking lot, and cameras were rolling. By now it was dark, and everything was lit with massive press floodlights. A sea of people pushed against the barricades they had constructed to get their best shot. Not only people from the press, but townspeople as well. I felt like a gladiator being led to the slaughter.

As I got out of the car, Detective Diskin said to me, "I'm really sorry about this. Let me put this jacket over your arms." He seemed so courteous and tentative that I felt a sense of compassion for him. How much had he been railroaded by the system as a new detective to do what he was doing?

Instead of being blatantly handcuffed, my hands were in front of me and the jacket was thrown over the shackles so you couldn't see them. It was a nice sentiment, but it did little to ease my shock and fear. I put my hands into my familiar meditation position and tried to breathe and center my mind.

*Get your head together, James, you can do this. You must.*

As flashbulbs popped, people were yelling, "Mr. Ray, why did you flee the scene? What do you have to say about the extreme heat? Why did you push people so hard? What do you think of your new bracelets?"

The reporters were in a feeding frenzy. My mind raced a thousand miles an hour, and I had no idea what was coming next. The only thing I knew about jail was what I'd seen on television, and that was not very pretty.

My heart pounded in my chest.

*Breathe, James, breathe.*

Like a person who can't wake up from a nightmare, I walked toward the front door while Diskin held me by the arm, showing the world his prize catch. The minute we were inside, he took the jacket off my arms.

The officer at the desk said, "If you're interested, I'll let you go out and talk to the press before we admit you."

*Are you kidding me? I bet you and everyone else would love that, now wouldn't you?* I had no desire to talk to the press. I had made no comment to the press up to that point. I never made any comment to the press during the whole process. I certainly wasn't going to start now.

They stripped me down. Searched all areas of my body including cavities. They took mugshots. Fingerprints. Filled out paperwork. I was in a fog, couldn't comprehend what was going on. I was given an orange jumpsuit.

Doing my very best to maintain control of my mind, I kept saying to myself, *You can do this. It's okay. You're going to get through this.*

And this wasn't even prison. This was just indictment and arrest and jail. Jail is *not* prison. I couldn't fathom what was yet to come.

Flashback to how my life had been just a year earlier. I had an executive assistant who took care of my entire calendar and scheduled all my meetings, and I flew everywhere first class.

I got off the plane and jumped into a limo. I took the limo to a hotel. I'd do presentations and make special appearances both in the media and on stages around the world. I'd step offstage (or sound stage) and go to sleep in my hotel room. I'd come down in the morning, get into another limo, go to the airport, and sit down in first class once again.Not now though. It seemed a faded memory from where I was in this moment. An entirely different lifetime.

What do you do when you're crystal clear on your purpose? When you know your purpose beyond a shadow of doubt? When you've worked and sacrificed for decades, and it gets ripped away from you? How do you continue when you're no longer allowed to accomplish the mission you feel you're here to accomplish?

I'll tell you what you do, and I'll tell you how you continue.

You discover a way to find meaning in your current situation. You find a way to correlate the pain and disappointment to the accomplishment of your purpose. You find a way to build the emotional strength and mental toughness to conquer.

---

*When you clearly know your purpose, you just don't quit.*

---

You take what life has dealt you and find a way to make it fit into the process and purpose and plan. You find a way to make it work for you rather than against you. You become bigger, better, stronger.

That's what you do, but it's not easy. Far from it.

I walked down the long narrow hallway of the jail with the guard by my side. We stepped into a room, and he said, "Pick up your bunk." I looked in the direction he pointed, and there was a stack of urine-stained mattresses on the floor that were literally a half-inch thick. "Pick up your bunk," he said to me again, getting frustrated and gruff. It didn't register. "Pick up your bunk, inmate."

I realized he wanted me to pick up a mattress. I also had to pick up sheets and a pillow and carry them all while my hands were still shackled. I had fallen so far, so fast that it just didn't compute. *You want me to do what?*

I bent down, picked up a filthy mattress, and dragged it to my cell.

There's a small trap door in the center of the big iron door of the cell. This is how they shove your food in to you. Once inside the cell, I looked over in the corner and saw a concrete slab slightly elevated off the floor. I realized that was my new box spring. I dropped the mattress and thought: *I'm still cuffed. Are they going to leave me like this?*

No sooner had that thought passed through my mind than the trap door fell open and the guard said, "Come up to the door and turn around." I showed him that my hands were cuffed in the front, so he uncuffed me and pulled the cuffs out through the hole in the door. This was for his own safety. They dealt with angry and dangerous men in this place.

Right then and there, all courtesy, kindness, and respect I had been previously afforded ended. From that moment on, I became an inmate. Not a human being. I got no favoritism. I got no special treatment.

They put me in solitary confinement, which I was grateful for because I did not want to be in a room with any of the guys in this place. Everything I'd seen on TV about jail and prison put the fear of God in me. I was now "one of them." I was now an inmate.

I picked the nasty mattress up off the floor and threw it on the concrete slab. I sat down on the bunk. There was nothing to write with, nothing to watch, nothing to read—just me and four walls. By this time it was late at night, and my mind was racing. I had no idea what was going to happen next.

When I had left Tom Kelly's office, Tom and Luis said to me, "We're going to be working to get you out on bail." My hope was that this would happen the very next day. False hope. Not a chance.

The State of Arizona set bail at $5 million. At the time, it was the largest bail ever set in Yavapai County history. They decided I was a "flight risk" in addition to being a danger to society. Five million dollars!

To put this in context, Luis had told me previously, "If this thing goes sideways, the bail will probably be around $25,000." Then they came back with $5 million?!

Here's how bail works: you're required to come up with 10 percent of the amount in cash. That amount is non-refundable. You're absolutely guaranteed never to see it again. That meant $500,000 in cash just to begin. Never to be seen again. The state and county generating revenue for themselves.

Then you put up security for the balance in assets, such as your house, for example. If you don't skip bail, and there are no extenuating circumstances, you eventually get your assets released. But once again, *not* the money.

By this time, I had already paid $500,000 in attorney retainers. In fact, I had paid *more* than $500,000, because once the retainer is consumed by professional fees, in the form of billable hours, you must replenish the retainer. If I paid the bail bondsman $500,000, I'd have zero money left for my defense. Almost all my millions of net worth were tied up in my now defunct business and properties that were in foreclosure. Assets with liabilities attached are not always the best of assets.

I couldn't make bail. The host of *Good Morning America* would go on record to state, "Here's a guy who wrote a book called *Harmonic Wealth*, and he can't even afford bail?"

He obviously never read the book to realize "wealth" translates as well-being, and he obviously had no clue as to the details of the situation. No one did. Nor did he care about the details. It was sensational news. If it bleeds, it leads.

It's easy to take shots from an uneducated and uniformed position. I watched this all unfold daily from the confines of my cell. The television in the common area blared loudly.

It's not the press's fault that there are few true journalists anymore. Mostly just sensationalists. It's *our* fault. If we didn't listen to it and buy it, they'd sell us something else. If we did our own research and called them out, maybe they'd be forced to do theirs. Maybe if we cared more, they would as well. They're just giving us exactly what we want.

I was in the county jail for the better part of a month, and I lost 35 pounds. Partially because of stress and partially because the food was horrible. I've always been very particular about what I eat. I don't eat bread and refined sugars as a rule. I don't eat starchy carbs. My resolve was set, and I was not going to let them make me eat things I don't eat. I exercised my will. *They're not going to break me,* I resolved.

The county jail kitchen has a daily calorie count that must be met by law. The easiest and cheapest way to meet the calorie count is to put four pieces of bread on the plate. Whoever heard of pancakes with a side of bread? French toast with a side of bread? *I'm not eating this crap!* declared my internal dialogue. *They're not going to break me.*

After I got over the initial shock, I decided I had to stay in shape for my own sanity. I did calisthenics in my cell, sit-ups, pushups, squats, jumping jacks, and yoga.

One by one, they would let us out of our cells for thirty minutes each day. They would start with cell one, then cell two, cell three, and cell four. I was in cell six. During my "out time," I was released into a common area where I could make phone calls. My parents had to put money on an account so I could call them collect. In that thirty minutes, I would rotate each day calling my lawyers, my brother, and my parents.

I also had to shower during the same thirty-minute interval, in a common shower in the common area. I had to stretch my legs and walk around. Thirty minutes, then back in the cell, no questions. No exceptions.

One day I called my family and said, "I always thought in my teens and early twenties that I would love to go to a Buddhist monastery and study as a monk for a time. I've come to realize that this is not that different from a monastery. The food sucks. The room sucks. The bed is hard. From now on, we're going to call this the ashram."

I was attempting to turn dung into fertilizer. This was the beginning of the mental games I would play to hang on to my sanity.

Sometimes it worked. Often it didn't.

There were ten to twelve cells in my cellblock. Two floors of stacked cells in horizontal rows looking out into a common area. Facing the common area on the opposing side was the guard desk, allowing them to constantly see everything that happened in the pod. In the common area was a television. I'm not a TV watcher and much prefer silence. Not here.

Inmates are notorious for watching TV—up to sixteen hours a day. The TV was constantly blaring in the common area, turned up full blast. It had to be loud enough for all the guys to hear it from their cells. The inmates stood at their cell doors and stared through a little narrow window and watched the screen in the common area. Guess what story was on TV constantly? Mine!

The press covered me incessantly on the television. My story was the biggest thing that had ever happened in Yavapai County. Everybody in the cellblock knew who I was. I was grateful to be behind the locked door.

My cell was on the bottom floor, which was problematic because every time I was on television, the other guys would be out on their own thirty-minute break.

One guy covered in tattoos and with only three teeth came up and pounded on my door, yelling, "Hey, sweat lodge motherf*****. What'd you do? Just lock them in the sweat lodge and fry their asses?" He laughed and pounded—*bang, bang, bang, bang*—on my cell door.

Then another guy would come by and yell, "You'd better hope you don't get out of there while I'm out." *Bang, bang.* As you might imagine, this was sheer terror for me.

They would run up to my window and yell something, then dash off. They couldn't get in, thank God, but they could peer in. I would sit there on my bunk and look at them. "Why aren't you saying anything? You scared? What's wrong, motherf*****?"

During my first week in jail, one day my food tray arrived and was pushed through the trap door. I noticed a piece of folded paper on it. I unfolded it and found a note saying something to the effect of, "Hey, motherf*****. What the hell are you doing messing with our traditions? You better not let me catch you outside your cell or your ass is mine."

*Breathe, James, just breathe.*

The whole time my story was on the news, the Native American community was in an uproar. Many of them were interviewed for stories, saying, "This guy is attempting to impersonate a Native American, and he's messing with our traditions."

I'm very respectful of all traditions. I always have been. Never once did I attempt to impersonate a Native American. The frenzy was in full swing, and everyone was jumping on the bus. A big Native American guy was incarcerated two cells down from mine. It appeared as if he had penned the note on my food tray.

Sweat lodge is a spiritual practice in *many* cultures, not just Native American, and in many cultures it's just a purification, much like a sauna. It's been around for millennia. The Native Americans have kept the practice alive in North America, but they are not the only culture to include sweat lodge as a practice. The Greeks and the Celts conducted sweat lodges, and many indigenous people in Peru and elsewhere did as well.

But the Native Americans took issue with the fact that I was a white guy and had incorporated sweat lodge into my event. At one point, they were going to file a lawsuit against me for trying to impersonate a Native American. That obviously went nowhere.

The Native American guy two cells down, incited by the press, was pissed. My mind started racing: *Is there any way we could end up being outside our cells at the same time? I hope to God not.*

After you eat, you slide your tray back under the door, and they come pick it up. I left the note on my tray, and evidently the guard saw the note and read it. Within a couple of hours, the loudspeaker came on in my cell. They could talk to me through a speaker box, and I could respond by pushing a call button.

"Ray," a voice said through the crackling speaker box.

"Yes?"

"Roll up."

*What the hell is roll up?* They never tell you what the prison terms mean. They never tell you what the rules are. You just have to figure it out on the fly—usually only when there's an infraction as well as consequences for that infraction. There are always consequences. After all, you're just a thing. "Property of the state."

Roll up. That might seem self-evident, but I was confused. *I guess they want me to get my stuff ready to go. Did I make bail? Am I out of here?*

I didn't make bail, and I wasn't out of there. After reading the note, they moved me to a different cellblock away from the inmate making threats. I wasn't safe. The last thing Yavapai County wanted was for me to get killed or harmed in their jail.

In the new cellblock, I was on the top floor in the far corner from the stairs. This was a big improvement because the guards were in the central common area watching at all times from the pod. Inmates could no longer just casually saunter by my cell, not on the top level at the end.

For them to hassle me, they had to walk all the way upstairs to the right, and all the way down a long, suspended walkway to the left to reach my cell. They wouldn't do that because it would be very obvious to the guards, and they would have gotten called on it.

In the new location, I was the very first cell on the top far left. Almost immediately, I got introduced to the communication mechanism of solitary confinement.

The fact is that most human beings can't stand their own company. Inmate or civilian, it matters not. It drives most people nuts to be alone with their own thoughts in silence. I've always enjoyed my own company. I've always been my own best friend. Because inmates can't stand their own company, they have to find a way to communicate with another person. Silence means they're stuck with themselves.

Most individuals in my experience, inmate or not, don't enjoy their own company that much.

## Calling Cell Seven

Each cell had one air vent above the toilet. The guys would jump up on the toilet and talk through the air vent to the guy in the next cell. The minute I was reassigned to this new cell and the door closed and the cuffs were removed, I heard through the vent, "Hey, cell seven."

I knew that was me, but I didn't want anything to do with him. I stayed silent.

"Hey, cell seven!" He kept yelling, "Cell seven!" I ignored him, hoping he would go away. *Please just leave me alone.* But he didn't.

Finally, I said, "Yeah?"

"What's your name?"

"Ray."

"Oh, I know who you are." *Great, that's exactly what I need. Here we go again.*

"You doing okay?" Something about his voice caused me to believe he wasn't ugly or threatening. "You doing okay?"

"Yeah, I'm doing alright, man." I was being very short because I didn't want to talk. I wasn't there to make friends.

I eventually learned his name was Ronnie. Over time, I also realized he was a good guy. This was the first of many preconceived notions that needed to be shattered.

Whenever I got out for my thirty minutes, I walked down the long walkway to the left of my cell to the stairs and down to the main common area. I had to pass Ronnie's cell immediately to the left of mine. He would stand by the door, and I could see him. Well, at least I could see half his face through the narrow vertical window.

"Hey, Ronnie. How you doing, bud?"

"I'm alright." We'd chat a little bit through his window.

I liked him. I felt for him. We had gotten there by different paths, but we were both swimming in the same toilet.

Little by little, he started asking me questions and told me that he was in for drug dealing. It's both interesting and sad that an average of 50 percent of prison inmates worldwide are incarcerated for some type of drug charge. Kind of a testament to the unrest and need for escapism in our world.

Gallup tells us that 72 percent of the people surveyed are unhappy and unfulfilled in their life and work. We're a society in dire need of redemption.

---

**The more things we have, the less they fulfill.**

---

Ronnie was very remorseful. He knew he had messed up, and he really needed to get his life together. He was scheduled to go in front of the judge soon for sentencing, and he was scared because he could potentially get fifteen or twenty years in prison.

I started asking him questions. "What do you want to do with your life?"

"Well, I'd really like to get an education, and I'd like to work with kids. I really love kids, and I'd like to be able to contribute to their lives."

I said, "Okay, write that down. Let me give you an assignment."

I started talking to him frequently through the vent, standing on the toilet. I was giving him life coaching in a situation where his life and liberty were literally at stake. As you think about it, in a very real sense all our lives are *always* at stake. Whether we like to admit it or not.

This was something many multiples of people had paid me to do with them. Coach them. Help them. Give them life and business advice. But the payment here was way more than that for me. Whatever value Ronnie got out of it, I got as much or more because I started to get outside of my own pain and offer something to another human being.

I was reminded once again that to help myself, I must help others. It's what my life has been built upon and will continue to be until the end of my days. It gave—and still gives—me meaning and purpose. Something we all desperately need. From my prison of pain, I transmuted pain into something that allowed me to have compassion for another.

Ronnie saved me in many ways. When my purpose felt yanked away, he gave me the ability to live it again.

## Limited Resources Get Resourceful

The supplies they give you in jail are ridiculous. Ronnie taught me the ropes. At first, I had zero access to books, nothing to write with or on, and no shampoo. If you want to wash your hair, you have to use soap, and the soap was the poorest quality, the water was hard and laden with sulfur, and the climate was desert dry.

I found out that if someone put money on an account for me, I could order pads of paper from the commissary, and the shipments arrived every other week. I could order shampoo and lotion. They also had a little book cart that came around once a week. I had to scramble off my cot at 4 a.m. to catch it, but given my discipline of rising early, this wasn't a big deal for me.

I desperately wanted good books to read. The pickings were slim. I guess I shouldn't have been surprised. Most of them were trashy novels I had no interest in, but I did get a Bible, and I went straight to the Book of Job—the same story Luis and I had discussed on our drive to Prescott. Maybe this would bolster me because Job came out of his situation a better man.

Job went through tremendous trials and tribulations in his life. He was very successful and had all kinds of cattle and servants. Then he lost everything and was in deep misery. He lost his family and even lost his health.

*Okay,* I thought, *I still have my family, and I still have my health. It could always be worse, James. Get grateful.*

As the story goes, Satan asks God to allow him to tempt Job, his "most faithful servant."

God tells Satan, "Job is my honored servant, and he will always love me."

Satan replies, "No, he won't. Let me prove it to you."

God agrees, and Satan brings it on.

At the time, what stood out for me was that the whole book is about Job going through this miserable time in his life, feeling sorry for himself, and getting angry. Then there's a point in the story where everything shifts. Up through chapter 42, Job is questioning God and asking God to vindicate him in front of the friends who chastised him. In verse 42:10 he finally forgives and has a change of heart. It states:

**"The Lord restored the fortunes of Job when he prayed for his friends."**

Wow. Tough medicine. Could I be a big enough person to pray for those who attacked me, wrote books about me, sold stories to the exposé press, and turned their backs on me? Easier said than done. Truth told, this was a spark, yet the fire took a long time to blaze. There were many ups and downs yet to come.

Was I not the guy on *Oprah* who had stated that true forgiving is the ability to state, "Thank you for giving me that experience"? That "All true forgiving ends in gratitude"? I was a long way from gratitude at this point, and while I didn't know it at the time, this was just the beginning. It was a long road with many steps forward followed by two steps back. And it was only going to get worse.

The end of the Job story is heroic because God blesses Job, and he has ten times more than he ever had before he went through the tribulations. Job goes through all these trials, and in the end he overcomes and is more successful than he ever was.

That gave me hope. But I had a lot of work to do.

---

*It's in our darkest hours that we can potentially find the greatest light.*

Challenge and pain reveal us to ourselves and show us what we're really made of. We grow the most and learn the most in the crucible of challenge. For it's our challenges that bring out the best from within us.

The Job story resonated with me as I was helping Ronnie through the vent. But I still had many individuals who were not here with me that had to be psychologically addressed as well, and many more yet to come.

## Finding Light Through Darkness

Another profound moment during the time I was in the county jail had to do with those personal care items I purchased from the commissary. I was not accustomed to the desert climate, and my skin was dry, my nose bled, and my lips were cracking. I had ordered skin lotion, shampoo, conditioner, and mouthwash—things we normally take for granted every single day. I remember when my first bag of commissary items came. It was very sobering for me.

I took out the generic travel-sized bottles and arranged them on the small metal shelf on the wall of my cell. I was setting them in order. I've always been a big fan of systems and order.

As I stepped back, I was so pleased that I had lotion, mouthwash, and lip balm that my eyes welled up. In that moment, I realized, *Here I am admiring these sampler-sized bottles of shampoo and conditioner. How much do we take for granted every single day?*

How many times had I stopped to be grateful for a bottle of conditioner? Probably never.

It was sobering. That moment was such a reset for me to realize how wonderful and blessed my life had been. The little things we take for granted every single day: a box spring mattress instead of a concrete slab, clear water, and fresh clean socks.

Every pair of socks they gave me in jail had holes in them. They were supposed to be white, but they were brown. All of them were used, recycled, with the heels worn out. All the clothes I had, including my boxer shorts, were used.

Never in a million years would I have ever imagined, even for a nanosecond, putting on a pair of used boxer shorts. *What the hell had gone on in those shorts? I'm not putting those on. Are you kidding me?* But in jail you have no option. They recycle them—they wash them and put them out again. If you want new, you've got to buy new. I was wearing used boxers and used socks.

## Ronnie's Redemption

*"A leader is a dealer in hope."*
**—Napoleon Bonaparte**

As I continued coaching Ronnie, things began to change for me. I could hear excitement and hope in his voice. I was giving him assignments through the vent, and he would complete them. We could only see each other through a thin glass window once a day, whenever each of us got out for our thirty minutes.

He would look in my cell and say, "Hey, man. How you doing?" We only communicated through an iron door or a vent.

The day before Ronnie went in front of the judge for sentencing, he was really frightened because he potentially faced a long sentence.

I said, "Ronnie, here's what you do, man. You hold the vision for yourself that you're only going to get the minimum sentence, and you're going to get through this. You're going to get out. You're going to get your education. You're going to help children. You're going to do all the things you've written about. Hold that vision through it all. Go into that courtroom knowing that's what's going to happen. Go in there with all humility and talk to the judge. Take responsibility. Talk from your heart."

I gave him a big pep talk the night before his hearing. We talked late into the night, both of us standing on our commodes in our respective cells, talking through the vent with a concrete wall separating us.

By the time I woke up the next morning, they'd already taken him away. He was picked up early and transported to the hearing. Later that afternoon, he finally came back.

I heard his cell door slide open. I heard the cell door close with the weighty thud that only a solid iron door can make.

Then through the vent I heard, "James. James. James."

I hopped up onto the commode. "How'd it go, man?"

"I only got three years." Three years was a big win for him compared to what he had potentially faced.

"I'm so happy for you."

I let out a big whoop for him and jumped up and down in my cell, as excited as if it had been a victory for me. In many ways it was.

Ronnie had done all this mental and emotional preparation and had been so afraid. Knowing that I was able to help him get through it felt good. Really good. I still had value to add.

## Let the Games Begin

While all this jail drama was going on, I periodically attended my own hearings. I was potentially facing thirty years. At this point in my life, thirty years was the better part of a life sentence.

When it was time for a hearing, the guards would come and shackle me. Pictures of me going to court in orange, shuffling along with my ankles and wrists shackled found their way into the tabloids. I would get to go outside for a moment on hearing days because the courtroom was in a building adjacent to the jail.

The fresh air and sunshine, other things we take for granted, were nirvana.

Barbed wire surrounded the walkway between the two buildings, and the only way to get from the cellblock building to the courtroom was to walk on the sidewalk outside. Every time I went outside, the press was hanging all over the fence waiting for me to cross so they could snap another photo of the "horrendous murderer." They would yell ridiculous questions designed to provoke. *Hey, Mr. Ray, are you enjoying your new hotel accommodations?*

I never said a word to any of them. If you see the pictures of me, I'm usually looking up at the sky. It was so brilliant blue, and I was grateful to see the sky and feel the sun after being in a little cell with no fresh air. I would take big deep breaths and appreciate the outdoors for those brief rare moments.

My attorney was furious because the hearings were a dog-and-pony show every single time. He said to the judge, "My client needs to be dressed in a suit when he appears in court. Can we obtain permission to get him out of this orange and put him in a suit and stop parading him in front of the press?"

The state objected and fought, but the judge granted permission. After that, the guards would take me out of my cell and down to a holding cell where I changed clothes. Instead of having shackles on my ankles and wrists, they put an elaborate knee mechanism on my left knee under my suit pants so I couldn't run. It was supposed to allow you to walk, but it went from mid-thigh to mid-calf. If you walk too quickly, it locks.

A lever on the side allowed me to unlock it, and I could release it because they didn't shackle my wrists anymore once they allowed me to wear a suit to court. I was walking awkwardly, however, because of the mechanism. The slightest overextension of the leg would lock the brace.

Often the courtroom was upstairs, and I had to climb the stairs wearing the brace. With every step, *bang*, it locked, and I would have to unlock it. Next step, *bang*, it locked again.

I lost so much weight that my suit was hanging off me like a parachute. My pants were literally falling down. This is not a weight loss program I would recommend for anyone. I had to tighten my belt so tight the pants were all wrinkled up underneath it. I was so gaunt that in one of the media courtroom photos the caption beneath read, "Being in jail is obviously taking a toll on Mr. Ray."

*No kidding, Captain Obvious!* I thought when I read it in my cell.

I still couldn't make bail. The bail bondsman would only allow $250,000 against my Beverly Hills home. This was the same house I paid $4 million for. *Are you kidding me?*

When we showed them the purchase price, the bondsman said, "Yeah, but we can't move it. The real estate market is upside down, so I'll give you $250,000, not a penny more."

Every time I went in the courtroom, it was packed with press, a complete zoo. My attorneys argued that $5 million bail was excessive. The DA argued that I had enough assets and that I could easily come up with it: "He's worth millions of dollars."

The DA hired an accountant to testify regarding my finances. It later came out that the accountant she hired was not even licensed. He was charged with fraud a few years later as I read about him in prison. You have to be kidding me.

Our justice system is broken, driven by politics, greed, and economics. These cracks and holes were affecting not just my life, but the lives of many.

My former controller, Alex, testified on my behalf. Their "accountant" said I still had $2 million in assets. But it was all tied up in assets that were already in foreclosure or in other financial trouble and therefore encumbered.

The prosecutor also argued that I was a flight risk.

My attorneys responded, "If Mr. Ray is ever going to rehabilitate his career and reputation, he's not going to flee because that would guarantee he could never do what he needs to do to get back on his feet."

This arguing went on for an entire month. All the while I sat in a cell.

After all the hearings, they dropped my bail to $500,000. My brother had to put up his home and his investment properties as security. My parents had to put up their home and their investment properties as security. I just no longer had the assets. Millions. Gone in the blink of an eye. I paid $50,000 cash that I would never see again, put up my house, and finally made bail.

My girlfriend at the time came to pick me up on the day I was released. What a glorious day. The guards brought my courtroom suit, and I changed out of my oranges. The suit hung on my gaunt frame. I felt like I could have been in a music video with David Byrne of Talking Heads.

At the little local airport, we had to wait quite a while for our flight. I was very uncomfortable because I had been plastered all over the news, and I wondered if people recognized me. I wanted to be left alone. I couldn't wait to get out of Arizona and back home to California.

Finally, we boarded the plane and got back to LA. At LAX, as we waited for the car to pick us up, my phone rang. Caller ID told me it was my financial advisor, Michael Thai.

"Hey, how are you?" I said.

"I'm good, man. I heard you got out, and I'm really happy for you. James, this is a hard call for me to make."

*One more thing.* Instantly, I thought, *What now? Welcome home.*

"Now that you've been indicted, my firm doesn't want to represent you anymore. It's not my decision. It's the firm's decision."

I had not yet even been convicted of a crime—I had only been indicted one month earlier and had not yet gone to trial. Yet all the banks had dropped me, and in a heartbeat I became the leper nobody wanted to work with.

Ironically this was the same financial services firm, a division of Goldman Sachs, that had advised me on things such as how much liability insurance my company should carry. The same Goldman Sachs that admitted they defrauded investors in the 2008 financial crisis. The same Goldman Sachs that was criminally indicted and had to pay $550 million in settlement.

In addition to being poorly advised, I was way underinsured for the work I was doing.

The families of the people who died in the accident had filed civil actions against me for damages. The civil attorneys were now coming after me personally, with a vengeance, because my company had only $1 million in liability insurance.

The company should have had much more coverage. I also had a $5 million personal rider. A new legal battle began between my lawyers and my insurance company to make this $5 million available to cover the civil claims.

Step right out of jail and off the plane and get hit with yet another sucker punch. Not even time to catch my breath. Keep blocking. Get back up. Keep going. Stay strong. *That which does not kill us makes us stronger.*

God, I was starting to hate that Nietzsche quote.

## CHAPTER 8

# Purpose: The Struggle for Freedom

*It's in the struggle that potential greatness is born.*

Most people don't like to accept or admit that life is a struggle. Some are too busy behind their smiley-face masks. In fact, they may do everything within their power to avoid even thinking about it, and hence the struggle begins.

A brief inventory of life proves that the birth of anything new requires struggle. Every significant breakthrough requires a breakdown of some sort. Breakdowns are a struggle.

---

*Every significant breakthrough in life is preceded by a breakdown.*

---

Whether it's the butterfly wrestling from the cocoon, the snake shedding its old skin, the baby chick pecking through the confines of the egg, the seedling pushing through the earth toward the light, or you forcing and squeezing your way to liberation from your mother's womb to be birthed into this life—it takes struggle.

And in this struggle to move forward and onward, in this struggle to leave the old behind, is greater purpose found and true freedom unleashed.

I was struggling.

The old identity and self-image of who I thought I was had completely shattered. Humpty-Dumpty had taken a great fall. I was trying to put him back together with tape but was not being very successful.

Realizing your self-image is just an amalgamation of the story you've told yourself over the years, and the opinions you've bought into from others, is sobering to say the least.

It's all ephemeral. Transitory. Temporary. We hear so much about the vast importance of "reputation." Your reputation matters little in the grand scheme of things. Your reputation is nothing more than what *other people* think about you. And this opinion can change in a heartbeat. It's not real or consistent. Believe me, I know.

Your self-image is nothing more than the story you tell yourself about yourself, based upon your interpretation of life situations. That's not real or consistent either.

---

*"Forget safety. Live where you fear to live.*
*Destroy your reputation. Be notorious."*
*—Rumi*

---

I was struggling to find something consistent and real.

I've been a student of Buddhism since I was eighteen years old. Given that I grew up in Tulsa, Oklahoma, the buckle of the Bible Belt, right down the street from Oral Roberts University, in the household of a Protestant minister, this made me somewhat unique. Maybe even weird.

I don't consider myself a Buddhist. In fact, I've studied most major spiritual traditions in my search for answers, meaning, and purpose in life. But now more than ever I knew deep down in the pit of my soul what the Buddhist sentiment of "standing on groundless ground" truly means.

I had nothing to stand on.

I needed to find my footing.

I needed to find purpose.

## Purpose vs. Pleasure

There's a vast difference between purpose and pleasure. Living your purpose won't always bring you happiness or pleasure. Face it. Deal with it. It's virtually impossible because happiness and pleasure are transitory human emotions. All emotions, whether pleasurable or painful, are fleeting.

That's not to say that living your purpose can't be pleasurable and happy. It absolutely can be, if you work at it and make it that way. However, it can also be painful and frustrating as well.

The ideas of "follow your passion" and "do what you love" require a caveat. Passion is the Latin word for suffering. Think of the movie *The Passion of the Christ*. The entire movie was about one man's willingness to suffer for something much bigger than his own personal needs.

Have you ever been in love? If you have, you know very well that it's often painful, frustrating, and *can be* absolutely infuriating. In fact, it can also make you want to throw large objects at the person of your desire and affection.

Your true purpose is no different. It's something you're willing to—and you're going to—suffer for. Passion. Sometimes you'll love the process and sometimes you'll loathe it. But you do it anyway because you know it's worth it.

Your true purpose is something for which you're willing to pay the ultimate price. And paying the ultimate price means giving *everything* you have. Redemption. Paying the price. In this case you must redeem your very life for this prize.

You breathe it. You wake it. You sleep it. You do whatever it takes to become masterful at it. You dedicate your entire life to it. You're willing to forgo pleasure and even suffer for it. Why?

Because it's worth all of that to you. And it's worthy *of* you.

---

*"Without purpose we would not exist. It is purpose that created us, purpose that connects us, purpose that pulls us, that guides us, that drives us; it is purpose that defines us, purpose that binds us."*
—**Matrix Reloaded**

---

Purpose is different from the transitory and material objects that seem to bring us pleasure on the surface. It's different from a bank account that can vanish, a house or car that can and will be sold, lost, or left one day. It's much different from a fleeting reputation or accolade that vanishes in the mist.

What we're talking about here is a true purpose. Purpose that remains through the highs and the lows. A purpose you're willing to pay the ultimate price for. A purpose to redeem your very life for. Before you run out of time. Before your life is gone.

Look, the hard truth is that we're all trading our life for something. You're most likely trading eight or ten hours per day for a paycheck. Most are trading four hours of their life every single day to watch Netflix, sports, or something else on television.

Taking a leadership role in your life is about ensuring that you're trading your life for something that's worthy of trading it for!

In many ways, the things we're consumed with are trite and meaningless. We've lost our big ideas and our compelling purpose to do anything great, other than economic growth. Purpose is much more than that.

Remember Elon Musk's purpose, "To save humanity"? Remember Alexander the Great's, "To unite the world"?

These are the things that move the very heart and soul. These are the things that free us from fear of the mundane issues of the day. Things that give us the courage to step into the arena and do battle with our own demons of self-doubt and self-limitation. These are the things that redeem our honor and bring us back to our true freedom and power.

## Free Your Mind

When I was in prison, I kept journals diligently. I wrote daily; it helped me focus and calm my mind. I wrote about the fact that while my body was surrounded by four stark walls, fences topped with barbed-wire, and guards carrying guns, my mind was not in prison.

In my mind I could go anywhere. I could be in Paris in a heartbeat if I desired. Then hop down to explore the Amazon. In my mind I could travel. I could experience. I could imagine.

While my body was in prison, my mind and spirit were completely free. I recall sitting in my cell, thinking, *They may be able to contain my body, but they will never be able to contain my mind.*

In that moment I realized that everyone is in prison. Every single one of us is in a prison—a prison of our own making. The sad reality is that everyone also holds the keys to their self-imposed cell. But most don't realize it, and some never will.

If I could sit in a tiny prison cell, sometimes shackled but always contained, yet find a way to make it meaningful and purposeful, then anyone can. We can all do more in our daily lives, wrought with challenges, to find purpose through the pain.

So why don't we? Why don't we make more of an effort to reach for purpose instead of dwelling on pain? It's actually pretty simple. We limit ourselves by external circumstances and overlook the keys we're holding in our own hands. Far too many people become their own worst enemy. Their own greatest nemesis. They're both their own jailer and guard.

It's much easier, even though counterproductive, to feel sorry for ourselves. At least it seems that way in the short run. Believe me, I've done this. I think we all do. It's human to think life is unfair. Guess what? You're right! Life *is* unfair. We have to deal with it. We have to pick up and get on with it.

The difference between the leader and those who never lead is how long we allow ourselves to stay in "poor me" land. It's a slippery slope into the depths of a victim mentality, and very few possess the mental fortitude and emotional strength to push back against the slide.

Fighting this battle is a daily process. I had to do it to survive mentally, and it's one of the most difficult things I've ever done. More difficult even than the physical training I went through during my competitive bodybuilding days.

Physical discipline is easy by comparison. Mental and emotional mastery are decidedly more difficult.

I began to crawl out of the morass of self-pity and "why me?" I stopped dwelling on how much it all sucked and focused instead on the Navy SEAL motto: "Embrace the suck."

I had to embrace it because it wasn't going away anytime soon. My only choice for survival was to liberate myself from the victim mentality. To find meaning in the meaningless. To turn trash into treasure. To find a purpose in my pain.

## Liberty Is Not Freedom

Years before, I read *Man's Search for Meaning* by Viktor Frankl. Frankl was an Austrian Jewish psychologist. He was also a Holocaust survivor. He and his family were arrested and taken to multiple concentration camps, including Auschwitz.

He, along with far too many others, was packed into a box car and not told where he was going. He recounts the horrific scene of arriving at the camp, being filed in like cattle, and watching the lines of other prisoners being led to the gas chambers. While he had arrived at his physical prison, his mental prison was his to choose or not choose.

As Frankl watched other prisoners literally curl up and die in their bunks, he came to the realization that there's a massive distinction between liberty and freedom.

Liberty is the ability to come and go and do as you please. In any prison, just like Auschwitz, you're stripped of your liberty but not your freedom. My liberty was stripped away. But freedom is always within your control and can never be taken away. Freedom can only be given away.

---

*You can't control life circumstances. You can only control your experience of life circumstances.*

---

As I thought back to Frankl's book, I knew I needed to focus on that difference. I had no liberty in prison, but I still had my freedom. The freedom to choose my own experience. In prison I was told what to do and when to do it. When to sit. When to stand. When to get in line. When to turn off the lights. Those choices were no longer mine to make.

I recall being in the shower one day when it was time for count. Once I arrived at minimum security, count happened three times a day, and we were required to be in our cells. I had come in from the yard thinking I had time to shower before count. Turns out I underestimated. I didn't have time. A guard came in, ripped open the shower door, and said, "Ray, you're not in your cell."

*Well, no kidding!* I thought in anger, not daring to voice it.

Adults don't normally think of things like the ability to shower privately as liberties. These are all things we take for granted. But not in this place. He ordered me to exit immediately and walk down the long run dripping wet to my cell. Once he "counted me" in my cell, I was allowed to go back down the hall and finish my shower.

The same thing happened again when I got violently ill. I had contracted a staph infection, in the shower of all places (I had placed my hand on the wall). Call me naïve, but why would you not put your hand on the wall in the shower? It never even crossed my mind.

Large boils broke out on my body. It took a month of pain and misery to get an appointment with a nurse. She told me, "Look, Ray, this is a filthy place. Whatever you do, don't touch the walls or the floor. If you drop *anything* in the shower, leave it!"

She gave me medication that turned my stomach upside down, and I spent the majority of the day, for several days, praying to the porcelain god.

As a result, one afternoon I was in the bathroom at count time, on my knees curled over the toilet with a stomach virus. In bursts a guard. My cellmate had told him I was sick, but it didn't matter. I got a "ticket" and lost my commissary privileges for a month. I could order no food. No clothing. No personal hygiene articles for an entire month for this "terrible infraction."

Most of my liberties no longer existed. I was a number, not a person. And numbers have no rights and no liberty.

Frankl believed that freedom is the ability to choose how you experience your life experiences. He came to this realization in a horrific place where people were dying, where exploratory surgery was being performed without anesthesia, where human beings were being treated like objects and tortured beyond anyone's wildest imagination. My situation paled by comparison.

He knew that he no longer had his liberty, but he also held fast knowing that he had freedom. Freedom to choose how he experienced his horrible circumstances. So Frankl put his energy into helping other prisoners. He helped prevent suicide attempts. He helped others to fight severe depression by encouraging them to reflect on happy memories and positive thoughts.

In the midst of horrific pain and suffering, Frankl found his purpose.

### Finding Purpose Without Liberty

I got a grip on myself. I knew I had to make my experience, no matter how unpleasant, meaningful and purposeful. If Frankl could do that in the confines of Auschwitz, I certainly could do it here.

Think of all the great individuals who have faced horrific challenges. The Christ. The Buddha. Martin Luther King Jr. Gandhi. Mandela. Each one faced imprisonment or other horrific life circumstances, and yet they found and held on to their purpose. I knew I had to find mine as well. There *had* to be a grander plan.

### Finding Your Purpose

More clients than I can count have asked me, "What do you think is the purpose of life?"

I believe the answer is to find your purpose and then redeem your entire life to live it and fulfill it. To be totally used up when you leave and contribute something positive and productive to the lives of others.

We're all hardwired to find our purpose, and we're all capable of finding meaning in our lives. Not only are we capable, but to live a fulfilling life *we must*!

---

*A purpose is always more compelling than a goal.*

---

As my head started to clear, I knew that if I asked to be a powerful teacher and leader in the world, which I had, then I had to continue learning from other powerful leaders. I had to be willing to pay the price.

All the leaders and teachers I looked up to overcame tremendous struggles. Nietzsche. Thoreau. Steve Jobs. Da Vinci. Michelangelo. Mother Teresa. And many others previously mentioned as well as not mentioned.

They all knew that this idea of living an "easy" and spiritual life is the ultimate farce and illusion. Those who have lived it—those who have really gone out and done it—have all made the greatest sacrifices. No one is immune.

---

*The greatest souls always make the greatest sacrifice. The greatest souls have always experienced the greatest suffering.*

---

Frankl and his sister were the only members of their family to survive the Holocaust. When his camp was liberated in 1945, Frankl decided to turn his experiences into a vehicle for helping others. He developed a theory called "Logotherapy" based on the belief that life has meaning, even in the most atrocious conditions, and that suffering has a purpose.

He believed that even during the most extreme physically taxing circumstances, there is still an escape—the spiritual self. The spiritual self is immune to external forces and circumstances. The spiritual self is the one that Buddhists call "The One Who Can't Be Touched." This is the true "I Am" that Jesus and others spoke of as well.

We're right back to liberty and freedom. Liberty can be taken, but freedom—much like the spiritual self—can only be given away. Never taken.

---

*"You may take my life. But you'll never take my freedom!"*
**—Braveheart**

---

Right then, I made up my mind. I was not going to let them beat me. I was not going to let them imprison my mind and spirit. Right then, I decided not to give my freedom away.

## Purpose Through Pain

I learned long ago that when we get outside of ourselves and focus on giving, versus getting, our life changes. It feels great to give, to support, to help. No one is a better example of this than Mother Teresa. She was a relentless giver and a literal saint. She gave to others because she felt good doing it. She felt good serving her God-given purpose, so as she gave to others, she also gave to herself.

We all must close the door on our pity-party and start focusing on others. Pay attention. When you start to help others, you feel better about yourself in a "good" self-centered way. Contrary to popular belief, being self-centered in this awakened way is powerful and productive. Being self-centered means doing what's best for you first so that you are enabled to then do great things for others and the world. Being self-centered in this way is *not* selfish. Far from it.

When you take care of yourself and follow your intuition, you have more to give. Many espouse thinking of others first. I suggest that as leaders we should think of ourselves first, realizing that you can't give what you don't have.

---

*When we take care of ourselves and follow our own purpose, we have more to give to others and the world.*

---

*Selfish* is something else entirely—being selfish is *not* me doing what's best for me, it's me wanting *you* to do what's best for me. Get the difference?

I can't tell you how many times I've had an executive coaching session scheduled—even to this day—when I'm not in the best place, when I'm dealing with my own struggles, and the last thing I want to do is talk about someone else's. Yet I push myself and make the call. And you know what? By the time I hang up the phone, I'm on a high.

I feel completely different. I feel better about myself. And I'm no longer in a bad place. All because I helped someone else.

So the question becomes, "Did I do it for them, or did I do it for myself?" The answer may be a shade of gray, but there's definitely some self-centered motivation and interest involved. I *know* I'll feel better when I get outside my own struggle to give a hand-up to another.

The same was true when I was in prison. I knew, especially on my worst days, that I would feel better if I focused on helping someone else. I had already decided that my purpose within the walls of prison was to become the very best person I could be in this situation and then help transform the lives of any I was blessed to serve.

## A Conversation with Skull Crusher

When I talked with the other guys in prison, I always asked permission to use their first names. Nearly all of them had a "handle," but I didn't want to address them by it. Most of the handles were associated with gangs or their former self-identity and everything that went along with it. These associations had long dark histories. I was doing my best to change that. Language is powerful, and if I could get them to associate with their birth name, it automatically put them in a mental state prior to at least some of the crime as well as some of the pain. I wanted them to start seeing themselves as the person behind the given name, not the person behind the choices of their past.

This was not only strategic, it was psychologically powerful. No one ever told me I couldn't use their given name, even though they often answered, "Okay, I'll let *you* call me that." They knew they had messed up their lives, some worse than others, and that they needed to change and improve. They simply didn't know how.

That was the tiny crack I needed to drive in a wedge.

Two of my cellmates were skinheads throughout my tenure. One of them was the former leader of the Aryan Brotherhood, angry, insecure men with a history of violence.

Justin was a former skinhead who previously ran the prison yard. He was the guy the largely Hispanic population called the Big Homie. Everyone cowered and acquiesced to the guy who ran the yard. He was a leader of this strange but dysfunctional and orderly culture. Even in this world there was a code of ethics. A culture heavily steeped in unwritten rules. Rules that when broken could result in getting "smashed" or even "ventilated," aka stabbed.

Justin had a big red swastika tattooed across the dome of his shaved head. I learned that his former "torpedo" was called Skull Crusher—for obvious reasons. A torpedo was the enforcer, the guy Justin and other big dogs sent to "have a conversation" with you when something didn't go as the big boss desired. Like any company or organization, this gang-influenced culture had consequences for all behavior.

One day early on Skulls approached me. I certainly didn't want to have a "conversation" with Skulls. No one did. My mind raced as to what infraction I may have committed. There was a whole laundry list of offenses in this culture from turning off a light in the wrong room to not giving enough respect by walking widely enough around one of the gang leaders.

The problem is that no one tells you the rules, and there are two sets of rules you have to assimilate: the rules of the inmates, and the rules of the guards. None of the rules are communicated, for the most part, until they're broken. You don't communicate with wild animals other than in the form of consequences. The same is true with numbers. I was constantly reminded that in this world I was 267823. No more. No less.

One of the Hispanic gang members once took me to task for "disrespecting him" by turning off the light in the laundry room. Full-on up in my face teetering on all-out brawl. A room he wasn't even in. But my turning it off required him to turn the switch on when he came in later. Which was "disrespectful."

For many of these guys the rules are just second nature. They're products of the system, having spent most of their lives there since their teens. They call it "being raised by the state."

So Skulls approached me and asked if I would take a walk with him around the yard.

I certainly didn't want to. But you don't say no to a guy like Skull Crusher.

True leadership is knowing when to take over boldly and lead, and, just as important, when to humbly follow. I followed.

Inside I was filled with panic, on the outside I did my best to maintain my composure. This was a 6-foot-5, 290-pound war machine. Within minutes he started asking questions. Surprisingly, questions about life. He told me how he was getting out soon, and after spending most of his life in this place, he had to make a change.

He actually wanted my input and advice. I was shocked yet pleasantly surprised and relieved.

We ended up walking laps around the yard several nights for exercise and talk. He asked deep questions. He wanted to know what I thought about life as well as the afterlife. You wouldn't expect this from guys in this place, at least I didn't. I especially didn't expect it from a guy named Skull Crusher.

My flawed expectation was a product of my own ignorance and judgment. People are people, and they show you all kinds of surprises. Great reminder.

When I first arrived at prison, I encountered shaved heads, tattoos, gang insignias, and tough talk. Now I began to see scared kids, frightened human beings—the same scared little kid I had been as I jumped, bowed, and scraped to the lawyers. The same scared little kid I was right now in this strange world.

Once I'd been master of my destiny, now I was the master of nothing but my own experience. Once I was in charge of my entire world, now I was in a world where I had nothing but my own wits, resilience, and resourcefulness. 267823.

I thought my only choice was whether to get breakfast, lunch, or dinner. But I was wrong about that too. Very wrong.

I had another choice, actually the ultimate choice—I had to choose whether or not to live. Really live. I had the choice to be free. Even within the confines of so little liberty.

Once again, liberty is the ability to come and go and do as you please. Here, I had little liberty. Freedom is the ability to choose how to experience life. My freedom was unlimited, and it always will be.

I reminded myself: *True freedom can never be taken away—it can only be given away.*

I took my freedom back one more time in that moment.

I no longer saw "me" and "them." Now there was only us.

Once I saw everyone around me, including me, as passengers on the ship of humanity, I also saw that we were all suffering. They were using heroin to escape their pain. I was trying to transform the world. They were watching TV. I was meditating. There wasn't much of a difference. Both were escapes.

## Tough Medicine

One day I called my then girlfriend from prison and said, "You know what? If I had the opportunity, I would run from this place. I would do anything to get out. But I can't. So I'm forced to be in my own fear and pain and deal with whatever I'm going through, whether it's depression, despair, anger, or something else. And it might be helping me see the answer."

"The answer?" she asked, confused.

"The answer is that there is no answer," I said. "The answer is that we're never *not* going to have pain and suffering."

One moment I was making millions of dollars, living in Beverly Hills, and now I was making zero money and sitting in hell. Neither situation delivered me the answer until I finally got to the point where I stopped trying to find the answer.

In fact, that *is* the answer. When you stop looking to change or escape life circumstances, and you just embrace it all and learn to find your purpose, meaning, and fulfillment within it, then, and only then, are you truly free.

This is not complacency by any means. The exact opposite. In fact, someone who is complacent could never reach the point I speak of—it's too difficult and takes too much work.

In a world of "positive thinking" and spin, I began to realize that true positive thinking is *not* expecting the best. That's illusion. True positive thinking is *accepting* that what is happening *is the best* for your development, betterment, advancement, and growth.

---

*When growth, improvement, and leadership are the objectives, sometimes what we perceive to be "the worst" is actually the best.*

---

Tough medicine, and certainly not for the faint of mind, heart, and spirit.

When you can just accept that life is hard sometimes, whether in Beverly Hills or The Hole, maybe hell can deliver heaven after all. Isn't that what all mythology implies? The Leader/Hero always descends into hell to fight his own demons, and once he overcomes them he's transformed. He ascends a new man.

We're all in prison at some level. Sometimes the very worst prisons have no bars or walls. We're mostly confined by the walls we build for ourselves. It's up to each of us to set ourselves free.

Even when life is hard, it's still a gift. Even when it sucks, it's still an extremely exciting adventure.

Purpose is the remedy that sets us free.

## CHAPTER 9

# WHO ARE YOU?
# COUNT THE COST

O ne day I was proceeding down the run to my cell when I saw a top gang member named Harley storming from the opposite direction and coming my way.

I had gotten to know him during my time here, and I liked him. He was smart. Really smart. I learned that many of these guys were. If they could just learn to channel their creativity in a productive direction versus destructive, they'd make something of their lives.

I stopped him in the hall and asked, "Hey, man, what's going on?"

Harley told me he was on his way to ventilate a guy on the yard for disrespecting him. He already had the shank ready in the back of his pants.

When you have low self-awareness, self-esteem, and don't respect yourself, it's easy to interpret others' behavior as disrespect.

I wasn't clear yet on what the other guy had done to disrespect Harley, but it could have been anything. Either way, he was infuriated.

159

As stated, I knew Harley was smart, but he also lived by a certain code of ethics.

I had earlier asked permission from "Harley," his handle, to call him by his given name. His given name was Aron, and he didn't have an issue with that. He had told me, "*You* can." Implying that this luxury was not afforded to others.

I said, "Aron, what did he do?"

"He called me a punk-ass bitch in front of a bunch of guys. I'll show him punk-ass bitch!"

I looked him straight in the eye and asked, "Are you a punk-ass bitch?" This was dangerous territory. I had seen guys erupt in the blink of an eye. But fortunately I knew Aron pretty well.

He kind of chuckled, shook his head, and said, "No." Then he said with a slight grin, "F*** you, Ray."

I had opened a doorway. Even if only partially.

"Aron, if I called you an overstuffed sofa, would it wind you up? Would you get pissed?"

"No."

"Why?"

"Because that's stupid. I'm not an overstuffed sofa," he said, laughing.

I didn't say a word. There was a silent pause that seemed to last forever. I could see his wheels turning.

"You see, Aron, the only things that bother us are things that we think might be true. When you clearly know who you really are, it shouldn't matter one bit what anyone else thinks. How much time do you have left?"

"Two years."

"And how long have you been in here?"

"Ten years."

"So, I'm curious, how much time would you get for stabbing a guy?"

"Probably about twenty more years."

I let that one sit there and simmer for a moment.

"Aron, I know that guy," I said, referring to another member of the Mexican gang. "He's getting out in two weeks, and he'll be long gone. You think you'll ever see him again?"

"Hell no! I better not!"

"Right. So is it worth giving up another twenty years of your life for someone who doesn't matter and that you'll never see again?"

I could see it click in. "No, I guess not."

Unfortunately, this insecure behavior of being consumed with acceptance and the opinions of others is rampant in our world. It's certainly not confined to a world of fences, barbed-wire, and guards.

What others think of us, and how others treat us, shouldn't matter if we know deep down who we truly are.

---

*Life is too short to get upset about what people on a free downloaded app, or anything else for that matter, think of us.*

---

The price to be redeemed is doing what it takes to become fully self-aware. In this way, and this way only, can we redeem our honor in life, redeem our self-respect, and then know how to truly lead.

This is one of the great lessons I've learned through my own pain.

I consider myself a leader, but there are those who would still call me a murderer. And that's okay. I know who I am. I know what the jury decided. I know I accepted responsibility and paid every single price that was asked of me by society and more.

At this point, if people don't like me, that's fine. If they have no respect for me, that's alright too.

I respect myself, who I am, and what I'm doing, and I'm going to continue. I'm not concerned with other people's opinions about any of that. It's not that I don't care. In fact, just the opposite. I care a lot! I care enough to redeem my entire life to be who I am regardless, to do what I'm here to do regardless, to help and support others, to become the very best leader and human being I can become. One chapter in this book is not the entire book. Likewise, one chapter in your life is not your entire life. It's just one chapter.

## What's Your Purpose?

Most people don't know their purpose. They have a job or a career, not a calling.

The single most frequent question I get asked as I travel the globe is, "James, how do I find my purpose? What's the meaning of life? What am I here to do?"

Every single week of your life contains 168 hours. A job, or a career, requires *at minimum* 40 hours of that 168. Yet Gallup tells us we're working on average at least 47 hours, with 18 percent of the workforce working 60. Even on the top end where you're redeeming 60 hours a week of your life for a job, that still leaves 108 hours for you to play with.

Now, if you sleep 8 hours per night, that's 56 hours of your *entire* life per week that you redeem sleeping. Subtract that from the 108 and you're still left with 52 hours per week to do something you deem meaningful.

Are you beginning to see how the "I don't have time" excuse is just that? An excuse.

On the other hand, purpose and calling require everything you have.

Steve Jobs was a multibillionaire. For some time, he had no furniture in his house. He could definitely afford it. When asked why, his answer was simple: he was never there, so what was the point?

Bill Gates worked twelve- to sixteen-hour days, seven days a week, for six years without a single day off. That's what it took for him to build Microsoft.

That's the price of a successful leader and entrepreneur. Count the cost before you begin a romanticized journey that'll be blown out very quickly and possibly blow up in your face.

You will have to sacrifice, pay the price, and redeem your very life for a position of true impact and leadership. The way I see it, the forces in this world that are trying to make it a dark and desperate place are not taking a day off. So how can I afford to?

But then again, I don't have a career. I've found my calling.

I don't work for a paycheck. I work for a purpose.

Big difference.

---

*For purpose and calling you must redeem everything.*

---

That's the price of leadership. But what's the big deal? If you understand through our discussion that we're all redeeming our life for something, you might as well redeem it for something meaningful.

For that's truly living versus merely existing.

## Stop Chasing Rainbows and Unicorns

There's so much romanticism and illusion surrounding the current idea of what it means to be a leader and entrepreneur. Millennials in particular want to be their own boss, to start their own business.

Not so fast.

Take a breath and ask yourself: What must I redeem in order to do that?

I've had to ask myself that question multiple times. I knew that if I wanted to be a world thought leader, which is my ultimate intention and has been for decades, I had to consider the price that came with it.

All great thought leaders have paid a tremendous price, and I've paid plenty. I've lost relationships, sleep, millions of dollars, my reputation, my home, many so-called friends, and much more in pursuit of my quest.

I ultimately lost my liberty.

Remember, there's always a price for the prize. The bigger the prize, the bigger the price to be redeemed. There's *always* a heavy price, and most people don't think about that going in. Trust me, if they did, many would never start. Why? Most people aren't willing to make that kind of sacrifice for their calling.

Because, let's be frank, most of us have a Netflix playlist longer than our list of life goals. That's a scary thought, but it's a hard fact nonetheless. Had I known just what that price would be when I set my original intention, I may have thought twice. I may have taken a deep breath and pushed pause. I may never have stepped on the path.

But once you've started, there's no turning back.

Never in my wildest dreams did I consider the price I ultimately paid.

Please don't assume I'm complaining or that I have remorse about this price. The price is the dues I owe. I'm just doing my best to shoot you straight and encouraging you to see things clearly.

Sitting in prison, I knew I had to get a grip on myself. One day I decided to take a brutally honest look at my situation and ask: *Who's responsible for this? Who put you out there in the media?*

If I hadn't previously been the media "Golden Boy" when the accident occurred, I believe the aftermath might have been drastically different. While nothing could or would change the severity and tragedy of what happened, while nothing would change the intensity of remorse carried for friends lost, it may never have turned into such a media monster.

I am responsible.

I knew, and accepted, that the reason I was vilified and crucified was because of what I created. I asked for it, I wanted it, I worked to build it. Therefore, I alone am responsible for the consequences of it. Both good and bad.

You see, your own redemption can be paid kicking and screaming and blaming and ranting. But you're *still* going to pay nonetheless.

I believe you come out of a situation like mine either bitter and angry, or you come out stronger, more aware, and grateful.

I choose the latter. Not because I'm a saint. Far from it. I've just developed enough wisdom over the years to know which choice serves me best. I encourage you to do the same.

You have your own situation right now. What will you choose? Bitter and angry? Or stronger, more aware, and grateful?

Choose wisely. The quality of your results, as well as the quality of your life, depend on the choice you make.

## CHAPTER 10

# ARE WE EVER
# REALLY REDEEMED?

I was released from prison on June 12, 2013. All I had left was ninety days of parole, then I'd be done. I would be fully redeemed, right?

Not exactly.

The press trucks, cameras, towers, and microphones were as thick as flies outside the prison gate where I was released. I ducked into a small shed inside the fence and changed into the clothes my brother Jon had brought me. Regular clothes. No more orange.

Man, things were already looking up and feeling better. I lifted my face to the sky and breathed the free air. *I can do without ever seeing orange again*, I thought.

I told Jon to step on the gas and just keep driving as we raced right by the press waving microphones and cameras. Some of them even jumped into the street and tried to block the car.

*Please, just leave me alone.*

165

The State of Arizona sent me out with the customary $50 in "gate money." I was so very grateful to have family that was able and willing to help. Many don't.

I came out of prison $20 million in debt and homeless. My gate money wasn't going to make much of a dent in that one. That would barely buy a tank of gas. In addition, I owed well over six figures in restitution to the State of Arizona.

The system puts you through living hell in prosecution, trial, and incarceration, and then they make you shoulder the cost of all that hell. You must pay them back for it. Talk about the price of redemption.

I also owed money to the families, in addition to the large insurance settlements they'd already received. Judge Darrow granted them reimbursement for their travel costs to and from Arizona for my trial as well as missed wages.

I don't begrudge them that. There's no price you can put on the loss of even one human life.

And yet I was broke.

Prior to my release, I applied to be transferred to California and complete my parole there so I could live with my family. I had seen them allow requests many times before for those whose families resided in a different state. The state denied my request. Arizona provided no quarter for me.

Without an approved place to live, the state would require me to live in a halfway house. Not an exciting consideration. My brother Jon contacted a former client of mine who owned a vacation condo in Phoenix, and she agreed to lease it to me for the ninety days I was required to stay in Arizona.

My brother made all the arrangements before my release and paid her the money. It was approved, and I thought I was all set to go—one worry erased from my list of many.

Or so I thought.

A couple of days before my release, she backed out of the deal. The condo was in a gated community, and she was afraid the other residents would catch wind I was going to be moving in. Supposedly, because I was so well known in Phoenix, that didn't sit too well with the neighbors, and my former client got cold feet. At least this was the story told to my brother.

Back to square one.

My brother came to Phoenix over a long weekend, and we set out on the seemingly impossible mission of finding me someplace, anyplace, to live. He and my parents had to get back home first thing Monday, so we had to move quickly. My credit was crap, I was broke, and because everyone knew me, no one wanted me.

Several places flat-out turned me down; others seemed to consider it then passed me over for a "more desirable" tenant. Even the real estate agent I was working with told me she risked getting a lot of heat if people found out she was helping me. To think that people thought this way about me was still mind-boggling.

Finally, we found a place, but just to be safe we put it in my brother's name. Then we simply didn't tell the owner I was there. Not the best option, but it was all I had left at the time.

With that taken care of, I felt like I was finally going to be able to settle down and relax a little bit.

Again, not so fast.

My California driver's license was expired, and the parole officer wouldn't allow me to leave the state to get my license or my car. I really didn't want to get an Arizona driver's license. I wanted no attachment whatsoever to that state.

Once again, I had little choice.

I hadn't cut my hair in the two years in prison, and after my release I grew a goatee. I didn't change my look because it made me less recognizable around town. My new rock-and-roll look was a far cry from my previous clean-cut business appearance. I really just wanted to be left alone.

Before I could even catch my breath, the lawyers had started up again, this time with civil lawsuits. One attorney, Bob Maganini, who was related to Kirby Brown, was still on a personal vendetta. He found another individual and convinced them to file a suit for damages. Almost immediately I found myself sitting in back-to-back depositions. Would it ever be enough?

Maganini's first pitch was that I agree to never write another book, never speak again at another conference, and never practice in personal and business leadership or performance in any way.

*Are you kidding me!?*

It just didn't end.

My criminal attorneys had been working feverishly on my appeal the entire time I was incarcerated. They felt very confident. With all the counts of prosecutorial misconduct (thirty-two to be exact), the suppression of evidence, the Brady violation, the lack of evidence beyond conjecture, and the monetary sanctions imposed on the state, they assured me we would win the appeal and the verdict would be overturned.

One morning I awakened before dawn as usual and thought: *Do I really want to continue this fight? If I win the appeal, Sheila Polk has the right to prosecute me all over again. Given her makeup she probably would. Do I really want to potentially drag the families of Liz, Kirby, and James through that again? Do I really want to potentially drag my family through that again? Do I really want to drag myself through that again?*

*Hasn't there been enough pain already? So what if I "win"; what does it mean to win anyway? At what point do you forgive yourself, the past, everyone involved, and just move on? Will removing the felon moniker from my name really take it all away? What do you want to stand for? Anger and bitterness? Or understanding and forgiveness?*

I decided right then that I was not going to proceed. It wasn't what I stood for, and it wasn't productive. I called my lawyers as soon as their offices opened and told them I was dropping the appeal.

They were not happy, to say the least. They truly believed in me and my case. They had spent countless hours and resources in researching and drafting the appeal. All pro bono because I was unable to pay them.

Two attorneys from MTO flew in from Los Angeles to Phoenix. Tom Kelly, my attorney from Prescott, drove in as well. These are all highly paid and skilled professionals who normally bill anywhere from $500 to $850 per hour. They sat in the living room of my rented condo for four hours and tried to convince me *not* to drop the appeal. They used every single gift of persuasion they could muster.

I respect them all immensely and always will. I felt incredibly indebted to them for going the distance with me as they had done. I listened carefully and considered deeply. But it was time to start making decisions for myself once again.

This appeal just didn't feel right to me at this point in the game. It was chipping away at the past versus forging forward. I called them the next day and told them, respectfully, to withdraw the appeal.

It was the first real full-fledged leadership decision I had made since the accident in 2009. Since that time, I had been bowing and jumping to the lawyers, to the creditors, and to the guards. Making that decision felt good; at the same time, it was frightening. At that point, my professional relationship with my criminal attorneys was done. I felt naked and without defense.

How interesting was that? Here I was, the guy who used to run an empire. I used to take a leadership role with team members, businesspeople, press, lawyers, bankers, CPAs, and a whole host of others. I made multimillion-dollar decisions with no qualms.

Where had that guy gone?

It's interesting how quickly something can be conditioned into you and just as quickly conditioned out of you.

I felt alone. Like I had no protection or shield any longer—I didn't. I had no one to consult with on the direction my life should take and the decisions I should make.

It was time to step up and take the power back. Right or wrong. A leader must make decisions with the information he has and fully accept the consequences of those decisions.

Once my ninety days of parole were complete, I went back to LA. Throughout the trial my lawyers told me over and over that if the case had been tried in LA, it would not have been taken to the extremes it was taken. It certainly wouldn't have been as much of a media circus, that's for sure.

When I crossed the Arizona/California border, breathing a heavy sigh of relief, I pulled over and took a picture of the California sign. I couldn't wait to get back to my home state of California. I was certain I was going to be welcomed with open arms.

That's not exactly the way it worked out.

The same issues I had in Arizona trailed me to LA. I had to find a place, but once again no one wanted me. My credit was still terrible, plummeting from a once-proud 850 credit score to a sad 500.

I was still broke, and as I soon found out, everyone knew me in California too—and they weren't exactly thrilled about taking me on as a tenant either. The media had worked its miserably magnificent magic.

After being shot down by multiple places, I finally found a nice, clean, yet modest condo that seemed promising. When I went to look at it, I pulled the owner aside in the garage and told him flat-out, "Listen, my credit is terrible, and you'll see that when you pull a credit report. I've been through hell and back…I'm not sure if you've heard the story?"

I gave him a brief overview of who I was, and he said, "Oh yeah, I heard about that."

"Well, that's me. Now I'm in a bad spot, and I need you to work with me." I figured I had nothing to lose by being straight with him. He was bound to find out sooner or later anyway. Google leaves no place to hide.

He said he would "think about it," which I figured was just a sugarcoated alternative to telling me "hell no." At that point, I truly felt like the untouchable. The guy no one wanted to associate with, much less take a chance on.

I had fallen so far I could no longer even dream of the place I'd fallen from. It seemed so far in the rearview mirror I couldn't even find it with binoculars.

I was driving back to my parents' small condo in Oceanside after looking at the condo in LA. As I drove down the I5 freeway thinking about the place, I wondered if there were even a chance I could get it. Not even back to San Diego yet, my phone rang. It was the owner; he had another tenant interested with "great credit."

"I'm sorry, I just won't be able to work with you," he said.

Damn.

I was back once again at my old stomping grounds: square one. Rock bottom. I was really getting tired of being there.

---

*When you hit rock bottom you finally*
*have a firm foundation from which to build.*

---

Two weeks later, out of the blue, the owner called me again.

"James, this is Richard. Are you still interested in the place?" he asked.

"Yes, I am!"

Apparently, the other tenant had backed out, and he agreed to work with me. *Here we go; I finally get a break*, I thought. Perseverance and grit had paid off. Finally, I was on the right track.

Except I had another problem I was dealing with—I had made the hard decision to file for bankruptcy. At first I had a huge problem with the whole concept of bankruptcy.

I recalled a seminar participant approaching me onstage many years earlier and asking, "James, they're foreclosing on my home, and I'm in a dire financial situation. Should I file for bankruptcy?"

I responded, "Well, that's up to you. I just know I could never do it. When I make a commitment, that's my word and to break it is a lack of integrity."

How could I do this now?

How things had changed.

My then-girlfriend, who also happened to be a financial analyst, helped me immensely with this decision. She said, "James, did you make your financial commitments irresponsibly?"

*No.*

"Did you make them with the intention of breaking them?"

*No.*

"Did things happen to you outside anything you could have predicted and controlled?"

*Yes.*

"Then the laws are made for a reason," she said. "Do you want to spend the next ten years or more paying off $20 million in debt, or have you already paid the price?"

I really believed that I had, and she was right. Laws are made for a reason, and nothing I was doing was out of the order of law. It was my right as an American citizen.

As I reflect now upon the interaction with my former client asking me onstage if she should file for bankruptcy, I realize that I had very little compassion or understanding. I just couldn't relate. My answer today would be a solid "It depends."

---

*Your arm is not long enough from the top of the mountain to give a hand-up to the people in the depth of the valley. You have to join them and make the climb with them.*

---

Life and business are not black and white. They're various shades of gray.

## Bankruptcy Hell

The head of the bankruptcy division in LA, Wendy Sadovnick, unfortunately took a personal interest in my case. At the time, I thought that would guarantee a smooth process, but man was I ever wrong.

My attorney, Marc Lieberman, assured me that this should be pretty cut-and-dry, and it should take no longer than about six months. Six months to close this financial nightmare and get on with my life. I was almost there.

Not so fast.

---

*When we think "I wish this would hurry up and be over with so I can get on with my life," we're neglecting to realize that this is our life.*

---

My bankruptcy took a year and a half. Eighteen months of pure hell and headaches. Let me tell you, it was beyond brutal.

Even my lawyer called Ms. Sadovnick aside and said, "With all due respect, I can't understand why the head of the bankruptcy division has taken such a personal interest in this case and why it's taking so long."

She explained that in cases of "celebrities and public figures" they were now required to be extra stringent and careful because of the extreme public nature of the cases. They had to be sure they didn't miss anything.

Trust me, she wasn't exaggerating.

What it came down to was this: the State of California just couldn't believe I didn't have some money sequestered or stashed away somewhere. The State of Arizona was convinced of the same thing.

Be careful what you ask for. When you get a full feature article in *Fortune* magazine on you and your business… When you get printed up in *Inc.* magazine as one of the fastest-growing and most successful privately held businesses in America and they publish your annual earnings… Those who don't run a business don't understand.

There's a *huge* difference between net worth and liquidity.

There's also a huge difference between gross revenue and net revenue.

All true leaders and entrepreneurs know this.

Many others don't.

As an owner and leader, we're an employee of the corporation just like all other team members. All that revenue is *not* going in our pocket. In fact, the owner/leader/entrepreneur *always* gets paid last.

This didn't compute for the bankruptcy attorneys either.

Another major problem was that they didn't seem to understand that all my net worth was tied up in assets. Yes, I had a significant amount of cash in the bank at one time, but that went like vapor before and during the trial.

When I loaned the company $1.2 million to keep it afloat, I had taken a line of credit against the value of my investment account. Once the bank heard about the charges I was facing, they did a cash call and immediately swept $1.2 million out of my investment account. $1.2 million, gone in the blink of an eye.

Now, I don't care who you are. Even if you're a billionaire, a million-dollar-plus loss in one day is a significant loss. And that was just the beginning of what felt like me hemorrhaging money every time I turned around.

I had to testify, under oath, about all these ridiculous little things like purchasing flowers for my mom on Mother's Day and meal expenses. Things that seemed inconsequential at the time became of extreme consequence to Wendy Sadovnick.

What impact did $45 worth of flowers delivered have on $20 million?

I was required to give them document upon document of every single expenditure and justify where every single penny went. It continued to amaze me that they expected me to know where every dollar and nickel was.

After exiting my 12-by-10 cell, I felt in some ways stuffed right back into one. What I expected to be a quick six-month inconvenience turned out to be almost as bad as the criminal trial. Scrape, bow, face endless questions that you can't answer, bite your tongue, breathe, and stay calm.

---

***Breath. Relax. Prioritize. Act.***

---

The leadership role I "took back" when I dropped my appeal was seriously waning once again.

*Keep the big picture in mind, James. They're just doing their job.*

There's a big difference between a leader and a manager. A leader is visionary and big-picture oriented. A manager manages the details efficiently and effectively. Think of Steve Jobs and Steve Wozniak as great examples of the two.

Yes, you need both, and they're both equally important. But managing details, especially financial details, had always driven me up the wall—and I had paid people to take care of that for me.

Now I had nowhere to run and no one to delegate to this time.

*Take a deep breath, James. This is part of your redemption. Pay the price. Even when it's hard and it hurts.*

Countless depositions stacked one after the other, so many arduous meetings, and one and a half years later it was finally over. Everything was written off. Full discharge. Thank you, God! A $20 million anchor from my now-defunct former life and business dropped off my neck.

You see, my former company was a C Corp. But in the early days, obviously with no business credit or history, it couldn't carry its own weight. All creditors, credit cards, banks, merchant accounts, and vendors needed a co-signor, a guarantor, and guess who that was?

Even though it became a profitable C Corp, all the bills JRI Inc. incurred were still guaranteed by me. Word to the wise. The price of leadership is high. When the company went under, they came after me for every cent. Full force.

You think this can't or won't happen to you? So did I, and I was obviously wrong.

## Next Steps

One more thing off my list, one more painful experience behind me. But it wasn't even close to being over.

In the meantime, while all this was going on, I was trying to rebuild a business.

When you're in the middle of a bankruptcy, no one will go near you. In fact, they won't touch you with a 10-foot pole. Trying to get business loans and merchant accounts and credit cards was virtually impossible.

That made no sense to me because, after going through bankruptcy, I was a pretty safe bet. By law I couldn't file again for another eight years. Yet no amount of explaining, cajoling, or pleading with the banks worked. Not even a little bit. I can't count how many times I heard no or got a denial letter or email.

I couldn't even get a personal credit card, much less a business credit card, and I was operating on a pretty tight cash flow. On numerous occasions I've pawned personal items just to stay afloat—the onetime multimillionaire business leader/coach and *New York Times* bestselling author standing in line getting pennies on the dollar for old clothes and furniture.

And my family, even my beloved elderly mother, has had to loan me money to throw me a life preserver.

Humbling brings you back to the heart. Humbling reminds you of what's truly important and what you're really committed to. Humbling proves who you are and who your true friends are.

## Is It Easy Yet?

Ten years later, I'm finally starting to turn a corner, but it's still not easy. That's not for any lack of working hard to continue to climb. I'm up at 3 a.m. almost every single morning, working at least sixteen-hour days. Seven-day weeks. I've come to accept it as my continuous process of redemption.

Yet I'm doing what I love and fulfilling my purpose in this life. So, while I work hard, it's hardly work.

I now know you're never fully redeemed. True redemption not only comes with a heavy price to be paid, it requires constantly working your way back and through that price. And the price continues to escalate.

---

*The higher you go up the mountain, the more treacherous the path.*

---

Remember how we discussed that when I was released from prison, I was so excited to finally be out I took a picture crossing the border from Arizona into California? I felt like the Israelites making it to the Promised Land.

But as you can now see, the Promised Land wasn't all that promising. I've learned it never is exactly as you imagine.

---

*Easy and great cannot coexist in the same space.*

---

It's not a cakewalk. It's not supposed to be. Easy is an illusion, and it's certainly not what contributes to great. Redemption is a lifetime journey.

Remember that you're always redeeming your life for something. This is a reality that cannot be escaped or denied.

I hope you choose to redeem your life for something worthwhile.

### Never, Never Give Up!

Another hurdle was working my way back into public speaking. No one would hire me because I was "too controversial." At the top of my game, I was one of the most sought-after speakers in the industry. Now I couldn't find one single person with enough backbone to stand up, take the heat, and hire me.

My media manager, John Ferriter, and I went to New York City with my literary agent at the time to pitch this very book. We went to four major publishers, and each one turned us down. These same publishers that got in a bidding war over my last book, *Harmonic Wealth*, and it was a *New York Times* bestseller!

It didn't matter.

They all basically said the same thing: great guy, great story, story needs to be told, but where's the "comeback"?

All I could think was, *That's what I'm trying to do here! The book is part of the comeback, dammit!*

No one was willing to take the risk. Once again, the press's dirty laundry was still hanging on the line.

After that trip, my literary agent gave up. Too much work. Not enough easy.

Fortunately, I found a new literary agent that wouldn't give up. He believed in *Redemption*, and he believed in me. After being turned down by every major publisher, he found one that also believed in me and this project. Then that went south too as the publisher hit hard financial times. The contract was off. My second literary agent dropped off too. People can only believe and work to a point before they lose faith from frustration.

I didn't. I refused to give up.

---

*The forces of resistance must give way to he who refuses to give up.*

---

Historically, the idea of a book advance ensured that you could survive without doing too much other work as you wrote the book. The publisher wanted you to focus fully on their project, which made sense. But not in today's world.

The publishing world has been totally disrupted and has changed immensely. While my last advance had been over seven figures, a fledgling disrupted book industry, coupled with uncertainty about me, guaranteed that wouldn't be repeated this time. I had to write on the edges of the day and find other creative avenues to stay afloat.

I'm beyond grateful that I finally found people who believed in the project and took a risk. *The Business of Redemption* is a step in my journey to my own redemption. A closing of a decade-long chapter of my life and "comeback," but it's humbling nonetheless.

It's almost as humbling as the realization that so many people who once clamored to hire me are now afraid to touch me. I've learned that the only way they won't be afraid is for me to keep pushing forward. And I must keep driving so hard, so long, so diligently that I can't be ignored.

It's next to impossible to stop someone who just won't give up.

It takes just one person, one brave client, one big convention, and then the floodgates will open. Of that I'm confident.

## The Dark Knight of Leadership and Performance

---

*Endure, Master Wayne. Take it. They'll hate you for it, but that's the point of Batman. He can be the outcast. He can make the choice that no one else can make, the right choice.*
—The Dark Knight

---

I thought the breakthrough moment had finally come when I got a call from a consortium of personal development speakers to come speak at one of their meetings. These were all former colleagues and peers.

"James," the voice on the phone said, "we really could have handled your situation better."

Yes, they sure could have. They were feeling guilty now and wanted to fix the relationship. After all, this was the group that espoused love, forgiveness, peace, and oneness. A group that championed helping and coaching and supporting those who need to improve their life.

The group leader invited me to come speak at their upcoming event. Now, I could have told him exactly what I thought of his group and his invitation. I could have told him how totally frustrated and disappointed I had been with the entire industry, and how they disappeared when I needed them the most. But I didn't.

I had long ago forgiven them, and I had done my best to understand them while sitting in a 12-by-10 cell. For my own sake, I had to do what I could do to mend the bridges and move forward. Not for their sake, but for my own.

A good friend and longtime supporter, Gail Kingsbury, told me when she heard I was going to speak, "Boy, James, that's pretty big of you after how they treated you."

I said, "I know, Gail, but it's the right thing to do."

Just like with the appeal, it was time to move on. We must learn from the past, not dwell in it. And we must integrate the learning to move forward and create a more empowering future. That's how we redeem ourselves.

You see, we don't forgive for the benefit of others. If they accept it, that's great. If they don't, it's still great. You've done what you need to do to drop the toxic energy, exorcize the poison, and move on. Another person's behavior is ultimately not about you, it's about them.

Lack of forgiving is like drinking hemlock and hoping the other person will die.

Not smart. Poison always kills the host. Through forgiving, you can literally turn poison into medicine.

---

*Forgiving is the antidote. Gratitude is the cure.*

---

I agreed to do the event. They asked me to plan a forty-five-minute presentation with fifteen minutes of Q&A. The message I wanted so desperately to get across to a room full of business owners was that this could happen to any of them. It doesn't matter what industry you're in. It can happen to you as well. Not one of us is immune.

We could get in an accident driving down the street of our own neighborhood, hurt personal property or a person, and be sued for everything we have. I know we don't like to think that way, but it's true nonetheless.

I wasn't an exception. Almost every person in that room did experiential learning. When I was with AT&T School of Business, we did a lot of experiential learning with managers and leaders. Even if it's just closing your eyes and meditating or visualizing, participants can always claim they were hurt or damaged physically, mentally, emotionally, or financially in some way by your business. This is even more true today than ever in the litigious world in which we live and operate.

Like me, they all had release forms signed and thought they were covered. Obviously, that's not the case.

I remember watching Ronda Rousey, the UFC champion, in an interview while I was in prison.

Interviewer: What you do is dangerous, Ronda. I mean, someone could get killed. Do you ever worry that an accident will happen, and they'll come back on you?

Rousey: Oh no, everyone signs release forms. We're covered.

Me as a viewer: Give me a call, Ronda, and let's talk.

I put my heart, soul, and lots of time into that presentation. I wanted and needed to impart value. That was my sole objective. I wanted them to hear my story, to understand I never imagined this could have happened to my clients or company. Just as they felt confident it would never happen to them and theirs. I wanted them to imagine the pain of losing people on your watch that I experienced and trusted they never would. I wouldn't wish that on anyone.

Maybe hearing it straight from me would prevent another tragedy. Maybe it would stop at least one person from thinking, *this will never happen to me*, and help them be more prepared. Even if it were just mental/emotional preparation.

Denial serves no one and catches us asleep and unsuspecting.

Less than seven minutes into the presentation, one of the attendees, a so-called "relationship expert," stood up in the back of the room holding a mic. He loudly interrupted me and said, "James, what the hell are you doing here?"

*Damn, is that one of the relationship skills you teach? That's interesting.*

Without missing a beat, I responded, "I don't know. My impression was that you guys invited me here to share my experience with you. Because you thought it would be valuable."

Another one of the group leaders, who was visibly angry (and I later learned was battling cancer), grabbed the mic and growled, "You're completely full of shit!"

*Wait a minute. Aren't you on the board of directors? Are you telling me you didn't know you invited me? Or did you just get overridden? Or is this just an intentional ambush?* My mind fired rapidly.

*Okay, I'm full of shit.*

*Breathe. Relax. Prioritize. Act.*

I grabbed the stool on the stage and sat down center stage. The leader of the group, the guy who invited me—the man with whom I had originally founded this group—was sitting in the front row, dead center. I looked him right in the eye and said, "What exactly do you want me to do now?"

He bowed his head and looked down at the floor. He said absolutely nothing. Not one word. This was his leadership move. Nice.

*Okay, so I guess I'm on my own.*

For the next hour and a half, they crucified me. I could have fought back, because I can call people out pretty well when I choose to. That's part of being a good life and business coach. Now was not the time.

This time I chose not to. I made the decision that I was just going to sit there and take it. To make the choice to be the outcast. To make the right choice. To shoulder all their pain as well as my own.

One by one, they told me what a sham I was. One woman even stood up and accused me of making my Spiritual Warrior attendee clients call me God. This had been sensationalized in the press. It was ludicrous.

We had been playing an experiential learning game I was certified to deliver at AT&T School of Business. It was a faux Samurai war game where everyone had roles and I was the proctor. There were warriors, there were sentries, there were ninjas, there was a priest. There were angels, and, yes, there was God. Everyone played a role. It was a life-and-business lesson teaching through a dramatic enactment.

Please.

"Do you believe everything you read in the press?" I had to ask. "That could not be more untrue."

The hypocrisy of the whole experience astounded me. I remember thinking, *I'm sure as hell glad none of you guys were on my jury. I'd have gone down for life. Maybe even gotten the death penalty!*

Just before I went onstage, the previous presenter conducted a guided meditation. The sole thrust of his message was, "We're all unified, we're all part of God. Part of the universe and one." Real New Agey, fluffy rhetoric.

At one point during my firing squad, I spoke up. I just had to call that one out. I looked out at the room and said, "Let me ask you guys a question. You just did a guided meditation about acceptance and love and all of us being one. Does that include me?"

Silence in the room. Their attempt to ease their conscience and mend relationships actually made things worse. Much worse.

I was a projection of their denial and pain and fear. Carl Jung once stated, "That which is most unconscious within us must of need be projected onto others."

I was their shadow. The Dark Knight of leadership and performance.

They were projecting, and I was their shadow on the screen.

Another marketing guy was scheduled to speak after me. He was not a member. He'd been invited to talk about how to gain more exposure on social media. Once my crucifixion was complete, he got up on the stage.

"I'm really happy to be here," he began. "I was told you invited me because I could provide potential value. I'm just curious, do you tell that to all the speakers you invite?"

He then turned to me and said, "I'm really sorry, James."

Obviously, he got it.

My price had been paid. I did everything they asked of me. Yet that was not enough. It was not about me, it was about them. It's *never* about anyone else or any situation, it's *always* about us.

---

*When we don't take absolute responsibility for our own lives and businesses, and everything that happens therein, no one else can ever do enough to fix it for us.*

---

In an earlier interview, a reporter told one of the family members, who had been particularly vocal and vitriolic, that I had taken full responsibility.

Her reply was, "Then why hasn't he paid restitution?"

I hadn't paid restitution because I was broke! I couldn't pay anyone anything. I could barely even buy groceries.

When I did finally start making some money, the very first thing I did was pay restitution. Even when that was done, it still wasn't enough. I get it. People continued to look for ways to ease their pain by projecting it onto others.

## A Light at the End of the Tunnel

Even though I'm beginning to see the light at the end of the tunnel, I could still be bitter and angry if I wanted to. But will that change the situation?

Will bitterness and anger change your situation? Whatever that may be?

No. Not a chance.

But then again, it will. It will only make it worse.

That's why instead I choose absolute responsibility (there it is again), gratitude, and forgiveness.

I encourage you as a true leader of your own life to do the same.

---

*When we forgive, we do it for ourselves, not the other person.*

---

Whether a person deserves or accepts your forgiveness is irrelevant; do it anyway. You still get rewarded. When you forgive genuinely, you let go of the toxic energy pulsating through your veins. That type of toxicity only hurts you as the host.

Forgiving occurs at three levels:

First and foremost, we must forgive ourselves. Forgiving yourself is the most difficult and yet most important. As we discussed, lack of forgiving yourself is only projected onto situations and others. When we truly forgive ourselves, situations and others don't matter.

Forgiving others comes second. We simply can't forgive others until we truly forgive ourselves. Again, the things we feel we need to forgive in others are simply a projection of what's inside us. Things we haven't accepted, forgiven, and embraced.

Finally, once we have forgiven ourselves and others, only then can we forgive the entire situation.

When I was on *Oprah*, I made a statement she asked me to repeat:

> *"True forgiving is the ability to say thank you for giving me that experience."*

All true forgiving ends in gratitude. Without gratitude, there's no true forgiveness.

## Gratitude Is the Cure

Many believe that "soft skills" like gratitude and forgiveness have no place in business. This is the farthest thing from the truth.

Studies in neuroscience now prove through neuroplasticity that practices of gratitude, forgiveness, mindfulness, and other things once thought to be the fodder of spiritual practices only have a tremendous impact on brain function. They literally change the structure of the brain.

When you change the neurons, you improve performance and productivity. Not to mention fulfillment.

At the end of the day, as painful and difficult as this journey has been, I'm grateful. I'm grateful for the growth, the awakenings, and the opportunities. It's taught me so very much about myself and life, and it's shown me what I'm made of and capable of doing. It clarifies beyond doubt that I know exactly why I'm here, and I'm willing to do whatever it takes to live that purpose. No matter what.

I'm willing to redeem my entire life, as we all do, yet I'm completely clear that I'm redeeming my life for something much bigger and grander than my own comforts or needs.

As much as it hurts that those who once applauded and praised instantly flipped to blame and attack, I'm grateful to be reminded that all things in life are transitory.

---

*The only thing that is eternal is that which cannot be changed, touched, or taken away.*

---

That unchangeable untouchable essence is inside of you, and has nothing to do with anything outside.

As much as it hurts that friends and colleagues turned their backs on me, I'm grateful for the gift of autonomy and self-reliance it has built within me.

I'm grateful to know who's *really* in my corner. There are relatively few. But they're a mighty few. That last part is powerful. I now know who will truly have my back. Do you? Very few people ever do.

My former Zen master once said to me, "You know, James, we always hope our friends and family will be there for us when things go sideways." After a long pause he continued, "They won't."

Tough medicine, for sure. Some will or may, but the mass majority won't. We live in a world that likes to raise people up. But we often love even more to tear them down. That doesn't make us bad people. It makes us human.

We all have our frailties and shortcomings. We all are desperately in need of redemption.

The reality is that everyone has their own issues to deal with. We can't expect others to have the extra bandwidth to deal with our challenges as well.

From that pain came compassion and understanding, and through forgiving I give a gift to myself.

## Seeing Clearly

When I look back on that painful period with lucidity and wisdom versus emotion, I realize what was happening. It was 2008-2009. The real estate market was quickly circling the drain. The economy was already deep in the tank. Everyone was struggling, especially those running a business.

Why would anyone want to associate with a guy who's got accusations and crap splattered all over him when they're already hanging on for dear life?

"I've got my own life and business to deal with. I don't have time to deal with someone else's right now."

I don't necessarily agree with that decision and behavior, but I certainly understand.

---

*Understanding does not equal agreement.*

---

Would I behave differently? I wish I could say yes with absolute certainty. The reality is, I'm not sure. I can't say exactly what I would do with 100 percent certainty. I don't know if I would do anything differently than anyone else did.

Don't get me wrong, I'd love to believe I would. I'm sure you would as well. But I must be totally honest with you and most of all with myself. And I trust you'll do the same for yourself.

We all like to think we'd take the high road. But one thing I've learned is that none of us really knows if we'll take the high road until we're standing at the fork. Until we're smack dab in the middle of the mess, none of us can say for certain what we'd do. That's real. That's honest.

If the tables were turned and I had the opportunity to help a colleague who'd hit rock bottom, I can only say I'd like to be able to. And what I've experienced might give me more power and ability to do just that. From experience, I know how much it would mean to them.

That's one of the many gifts of redemption and fully paying the price.

## Continuing to Pay the Price

I recently "celebrated" the six-year anniversary of my release. A lot of water has passed under the bridge during that time. A lot of situations have occurred, some pleasant and some not so pleasant. I've learned a tremendous amount about myself, about life, about others, about the legal system, and so many other things.

I also know that my work isn't done—far from it—and there's plenty left to do. I've paid my price in countless ways, and I'm still paying. But I've also learned that there's still more to be paid and always will be.

One thing is for certain: I will *never* come to the end of my life and say, "Damn, that was boring."

For the true purpose of life is to live—really live! Not merely exist.

And the greatest pain is the pain of regret.

My path to redemption, your path to redemption, has no end. It's constant, it's hard work, but it's rewarding. It's also filled with frustrations and setbacks; that's just part of the process.

Step up, buckle up, and let's get on with it.

## CHAPTER 11

# THE WORLD NEEDS
# NEW LEADERSHIP

U ltimately this story is not about me, it's about you.

Never has there been a stronger and deeper need for a reemergence of more true leaders in our world.

Remember, please, that true leadership has *nothing* to do with title or position. Nothing to do with followers or popularity. Nothing to do with whether you're a business owner or just an owner of your life.

Leadership is about self-awareness, autonomy, and deep commitment to something far beyond our own personal creature comforts and needs. Leadership is about transforming the world.

---

*"Those who are crazy enough to think they can change the world usually do."*
—**Steve Jobs**

---

When I think of the true leaders who have inspired nations through their willingness to pay the price of redemption, I think of people like Socrates, Jesus the Christ, Gautama Buddha, Alexander the Great, Thomas Jefferson, Mahatma Gandhi, Mother Teresa, John F. Kennedy, Martin Luther King Jr., Rosa Parks, Nelson Mandela, Steve Jobs, and Elon Musk, just to name a few.

---

*Don't ask what the world needs. Ask what makes you come alive, and go do it. Because what the world needs is people who have come alive.*
**—Howard Thurman**

---

What's your Powerful Transforming Purpose (PTP) worthy of redeeming your very life for?

What's your cause of great magnitude?

For redeeming your entire life for something of this nature is what builds true leadership.

It won't be easy. It's not supposed to be easy.

But it will be fulfilling and meaningful.

The path will be fraught with danger, self-doubt, and often downright exhaustion. But the inspiration and contribution you leave behind will be that of which legacies are made.

---

*"If you make yourself more than just a man, if you devote yourself to an ideal, and if they can't stop you, then you become something else entirely. You become legend."*
**—Batman Begins**

---

I challenge you to choose to see everything that falls in your path as a gift and experience. Part of the price you must redeem to fulfill your purpose. An opportunity to grow, expand, and become more masterful.

This goes for all things good and all things bad. For it's in the furnace and fire that steel is forged. The crucible of challenge is where you learn and grow the most, and it's in your most difficult struggles that potential greatness is born.

Life can be tough.

Business can be tougher.

But as Nietzsche so wisely stated, "That which does not kill us makes us stronger."

Every single thing in your life and business is here to serve you, even when it's not wrapped in a pretty package. Sometimes even more so when it's not in a pretty package.

True leaders know this, and they use everything, versus being used *by* it.

When you find your purpose, choose to lead your own life and give your all to it. Then the journey begins.

Michael J. Fox once stated about his battle with Parkinson's, "My situation is a gift. A gift wrapped in pain but a gift nonetheless."

Each period of our lives, good and bad, is a gift. We simply must choose to see it this way.

In this way do you become a true leader.

In this way do you make your own unique dent in the universe.

In this way do you pay the price, and therein lies your redemption.

The path to redemption is endless. The path to redemption is challenging, dangerous, frustrating, and many times painful. But that's the price for the prize. That's the price you must pay for your purpose. And you alone can *choose* to do so.

Can you make that choice fully and authentically?

Will you?

# EPILOGUE

In November 2017, I went back to Sedona for the first time with my soon-to-be wife, Bersabeh (Bear), the woman I love dearly and who had been my rock through the arduous climb we'd made together in the last four years. Bear decided to gift me with a trip of healing and closure for my birthday, and this trip was that gift.

We revisited the site of the accident together, the site of so much tragedy and loss. Four years had passed since my release from prison. It was time to turn the page.

As the desert air hung hot and dry around me, I was reminded of my time in the Sinai Peninsula at Wadi Maktub. The energy was similarly heavy. Both Bear and I could feel it, and even our little dog Flow was uneasy, sensing something either in me or this place. Maybe both. She jumped up on my leg, scratching to be picked up off the warm and barren sand.

With tears flowing down both our faces, I sank to my knees in this place of past pain. Bear followed.

I said a prayer for James, Liz, and Kirby. I said a prayer for all those who'd been hurt by the event, including their families.

And I said a prayer for me—making my peace at last with the place that had changed so many lives so dramatically.

After the ceremony, we drove off the Angel Valley Ranch property in silence. It felt as if a tremendous weight was pulled from my mind, body, and soul as we headed the miles back into town.

Later that afternoon we hiked up among the Red Rocks of Boynton Canyon. Night falls fast in the desert, the sky bright blue one minute and then black the next. I knew we only had a few minutes. Twilight was already sweeping like a blanket over the cloudless expanse above.

Sitting on the edge of this spectacular wonder of nature, we found an outcropping in the canyon where we could be alone in silence for a few moments.

Hugging Bear tightly to me, I raised my face to the sky and closed my eyes.

And breathed.

And gave thanks.

# 29 Lessons Learned for Both Life and Business

1. When your entire life appears to be falling apart, it's just coming together on a grander scale.

2. Positive thinking is not expecting the best—that's illusion. True positive thinking is accepting that what is happening is the best.

3. You don't want an easier life. What you want is greater strength, capacity, and capability to get through the challenges life brings. Increase your bandwidth.

4. Always expect the best, and realize that often what you perceive to be the worst actually is the best for your development, advancement, and growth.

5. Ask for more. When I felt as if I just couldn't take it anymore, my Zen master told me, "James, ask for more." You have infinite capacity, and like a muscle it only grows by pushing its limits.

6. Pain is your friend. The mother of all growth.

193

7. Pain is a natural part of life. Suffering is a choice. Suffering results when we try to suppress, escape, or deny pain. Pain is not a signal to suffer, it's a signal to grow.

8. It's possible to transform pain into medicine. It's not easy, but that's how champions and true leaders are built.

9. Stress and pressure are not your enemies. Diamonds grow under duress.

10. If you're going to play a big game, and grow a bigger reach and business, expect bigger problems. And more of them, not less.

11. The things you fear the most when confronted bring out the best within you. Your greatest opportunity resides just beyond your greatest fear.

12. True wealth is not what you have. True wealth is what you're left with when all you have is gone.

13. Most people do the best they can with the resources they have available to them. The challenge is often not a challenge of character, but rather a challenge of knowledge, experience, and resources.

14. If your friends and family aren't there for you in a storm, it's not that they're bad people. They're probably just too consumed with dealing with their own storm to take on yours. Understand them. Forgive them.

15. Even those few who will stand with you in a storm have their limits. We all can only do the best we can with what we have.

16. There are no bad teams, people, or circumstances. There are only bad leaders.

17. True leaders take absolute responsibility for every single thing in their life and business. This concept, expanded to the level of absurd, allows for life and business to be a bio-feedback mechanism for growth and improvement.

18. Forgiving is done for you, not the other person. True forgiving is the ability to say, "Thank you *for giving* me that experience." If you're not grateful, you're not there yet.

19. Refusing to forgive is like drinking hemlock and thinking the other person will die. The poison always kills the host.

20. We're all flawed and imperfect. You must learn to love yourself regardless. Forgiving starts with you first, others second.

21. There are three levels where forgiving must be practiced (thank you *for giving* me that experience): 1) yourself first, 2) others, 3) situations and circumstances.

22. Mistakes are our greatest teachers. They show us our failures and shortcomings. They show us where we have opportunities to grow.

23. All challenges and pain are relative. Everyone's hardest thing is their hardest thing.

24. Every breakthrough is almost invariably preceded by a breakdown.

25. Life is not meant for safety and security. Life is meant to be lived fully and completely.

26. True vision, belief, character, and conviction are defined and established when you're being hit by a tsunami.

27. Relax, nothing is in control. You have no control. However, you do have influence, choice, and freedom.

28. The greatest control is having no need for control. Ironically, this takes a lot of self-control.

29. When you find meaning and purpose, life becomes more engaging, alive, and complete. True fulfillment ensues. Regardless of what life throws your way, you conquer versus quit.

# ABOUT THE AUTHOR

James Arthur Ray is the author of six internationally bestselling books, including his *New York Times* bestseller *Harmonic Wealth: The Secret to Attracting the Life You Want*, and a co-author and contributor to *The Secret*.

Ray has worked with over one million people from 145 countries through his audio, video, coaching, and life and business leadership programs. More than one million people have attended his live events worldwide.

James Arthur Ray's company hit the Inc. 500 list in 2009 as one of the fastest-growing, most successful privately held companies in the United States, and possibly the world.

In 2007 he was awarded the distinguished Toastmasters award for Outstanding Communication and Leadership. His book *Harmonic Wealth* was voted as one of the top celebrity reads by *People* magazine in 2008. *Fortune* magazine wrote a full feature article on him in 2008, heralding him as the new frontrunner in leadership and performance.

Ray has appeared numerous times on *Larry King Live*, *Piers Morgan*, *The Today Show*, *Good Morning America*, CNN, and *Oprah*.

After rising to the pinnacle of his profession, he and his company were involved in a tragic accident in 2009, and he lost everything. Since that time, he has applied the same strategies he taught his clients for decades to rebuild his own life and business and to come back strong.

Ray's life story is told in the CNN documentary *Enlighten Us*, released on CNN in 2016 and now on Netflix.

Because of his experience in building from humble beginnings and scratch, as well as rebuilding after hitting rock bottom post crises, Ray has the unique experience and ability to help those at the top, those on the climb, and those who must put their life back together to get up and climb again.

In his mission to positively impact a minimum of one billion lives and businesses worldwide, Ray continues to bring his experience, resilience, adaptability, and wisdom to all those he's blessed to serve and support.

James Arthur Ray resides in Henderson, Nevada.

**For information regarding his coaching,**
**business consulting, appearances, products, and resources,**
**visit www.jamesray.com**

**Interested in attending a live Leadership Experience with James? Go here:**
**https://www.jamesray.com/upcoming-events/**

Printed in the USA
CPSIA information can be obtained
at www.ICGtesting.com
JSHW022333140824
68134JS00019B/1464